The Korean

Single and Obese: Then Kimchi Changed Everything!

The Korean

Single and Obese: Then Kimchi Changed Everything!

AFRICA BYONGCHAN YOON

BLACKYOONICORN
PRESS

The Korean: Single and Obese: Then Kimchi Changed Everything

Published by BLACKYOONICORN PRESS

Library of Congress Control Number: 2021932545

ISBN (hardcover): 9781662910586
ISBN (paperback): 9781662910593
eISBN: 9781662910609

CONTENTS

DEDICATION

*For my sweet Korean mommies who showed
me that true love in friendship transcends race.
I will never forget how you have welcomed me.
Thank you for the prayers, ideas, phone calls,
introductions, lunches, dinners, late-night texts,
recipes, DMs, and more. I love you ummas.*

FOREWORD

By Marja Vongerichten

As the culinary influence of Korean cuisines begins to spread globally, so now will we begin to hear stories of the places near and far that it reached. While traditionally the cuisine tells the story of Korean people born in North and South Korea, non-Koreans now will begin to add to the tapestry of what Korean food means to them. Such is the story you are about to read involving a girl from Cameroon who, at age six, eats kimchi for the first time, connects with it as a teen, and then a decade later, it saves her life. The deep impact felt, which keeps the cuisine in her daily life, is the tip of the iceberg as we begin to see just how far the red spice of gochugaru, the Asian pear, and the bubbling flavors of Korean food have traveled.

While born in Korea, I personally discovered my own connection to it much later in my life.

I was born in South Korea, adopted at the age of three, and raised in America by my adopted parents. I always had memories of my time in Korea, but they were faded pieces floating around in my mind. I was able to find my birth mother at the age of 19. From the meal she served me on the first day that we met, after seventeen years of being apart, I realized my connection to Korea was always within me; it was in my taste buds and, from the first bite, a wealth of knowledge flooded back to me—a knowledge that I needed to explore. I became obsessed with every Korean flavor like I was trying to reclaim a memory in my mind through every bite.

Fast-forward to about twenty years later, when I received the opportunity to be the host of a television docuseries for the Public Broadcasting System (PBS) called *Kimchi Chronicles*. It is about my personal story and journey into Korean food and culture. The show aired in 140 countries and gained a long reach—a reach that brings me to 2018 when I started getting positive and encouraging messages from this woman named Africa Yoon.

She contacted me and told me the impact the show had on her life and said she wanted to thank me. We soon became fast virtual friends. Little did I know she was reaching out to me during a difficult time in her life. We remained in touch and, in the summer of 2020, began to communicate more regularly. I was quite impressed with a new Facebook group that Africa started called "Korean Cooking Friends." I thought it was such a nice forum to bring about awareness and togetherness about a love for Korean cooking. Africa and I share a mutual passion for Korean food and culture, and it is reflected in the way we live our lives.

In this book, she shares her journey from her younger years with bits and dabbles of Korean elements throughout her life, as the daughter of an ambassador to the United Nations from Cameroon to her deeper knowledge and drive to learn about Korean food and all the advantages and health benefits it can lend to one's overall health. There are many references to Korean words, foods, and customs. You may learn a thing or two!

Africa's journey took me from struggles with her weight, relationships, and her tenacity to get what she wants and without apology. She shares the vulnerability in each facet of her life, from dating to running miles and miles, finding true love, health issues, tremendous loss, and ultimate happiness along the way. This book is a story of love, perseverance, ingenuity, self-reflection, self-help, and a belief in the power of one's own strength and inner compass.

I hope you are inspired just as I was after reading this book. Wishing you well with your dreams, Africa Yoon. As Koreans say... FIGHTING!! (Keep fighting, keep going!)

PREFACE

It all started when that *halmoni* called me fat in H Mart. I can't believe where I ended up more than a decade later. Today I live in Oahu, Hawaii, and the lessons from that time are still ever-present. Yesterday, I realized it had been a while since I felt my emotions get the best of me. The tears were streaming down my cheeks; they tasted salty as they hit my tongue. Something about the salt and living at the beach made me crave a similar taste to soothe my soul. I grabbed a jar from the top of my kimchi fridge. As my hand clutched the contents, I heard one of my favorite sounds on Earth—the sound of dried seaweed crunching. I intended to make *miyeok-guk*, a Korean soup that tiptoes behind a Korean woman throughout her life—from the day she gives birth and every birthday until the day she dies. It is said that Korean women are in tune with nature, including the sea. This tradition began when they found out that whales used seaweed to replenish themselves after birth. It was observed that when mother whales gave birth, there was less *miyeok*—the Korean word for seaweed—in the ocean. The *umma* whale eats it all up to become strong again, and that is how that tradition began.

After a Korean woman gives birth during a period known as *sanhujori*, which lasts a month after delivery, she drinks this soup full of calcium and iodine to restore her body. She then drinks it each birthday after, and so do her children, honoring her pain and work in bringing them to Earth.

So how does it come to pass that a woman born in West Central Africa comes to have *miyeok-guk* as the soup that comforts her soul on a hard day? It was only yesterday, as I reached for it, my face awash with saltwater tears, that I realized my comfort food had become something I was never fed as a young girl. As the salty miyeok hit my tongue and warmed me, I realized Korean food had become more than just a part of my life—it is a thread in my soul. There is only one way that two things can blend together while remaining autonomous; this can only happen with love, which I have in abundance.

1

I called the Green Kitchen Restaurant for dinner. John, the owner, picked up and took my order. I ordered a cheeseburger with bacon. He asked me if there was anything else. "Yes, I'll order another cheeseburger for my friend who does not want bacon." There was no friend. Years later, John told me he knew there was no friend because I went from being a skinny girl to the size of two people!

When the burgers arrived, I tipped the delivery man ten dollars; he worked so hard. I warmed the leftover bulgogi from lunch on the gas stove. Bulgogi literally translates in Korean to *bul*, fire, and *gogi*, meat. It is the most famous of the Korean BBQ foods. It has a history that stretches back to the Goguryeo era in Korea, which began in 37 BC when it was initially called *maekjok* and eaten on a skewer. It evolved into what it is now—a thin slice of top sirloin marinated in Asian pear, rice wine, garlic, brown sugar, soy sauce, and black pepper. After a few hours, the meat dancing with flavor is ready for preparation.

At a Korean restaurant, the marinated meat is brought to you raw. You prepare it on a grill embedded in the center of the table. At home, you can prepare it on the stovetop or a mini grill. (Many Korean families have a mini grill placed in the middle of their own table.) If you don't order enough raw meat at a Korean

BBQ restaurant, they prepare it for you in the kitchen and bring it to the table.

I opened the burger, took out the bacon, chopped it, and mixed it in the pan with the bulgogi. Then I took the mixture, wrapped it in a lettuce leaf with some *gochujang*, and put it back in the burger. The gochujang was sweet with some subtle heat. It's often described as Korean ketchup by people too lazy to tell you what it actually is. It makes everything sing. Gochujang is a fermented chili paste made with Korean chili powder, glutinous rice named *chappsal*, a fermented soybean powder called *meju*, malt called *yeotgireum*, and salt. To call it ketchup insults its traditional history. It was fermented for years in earthenware. Every step of the painstaking process results in turning everything it touches—including my simple burger that night—into a little pocket of Heaven.

Some sauce dripped down my arm; I hadn't even left the kitchen. I was just eating while standing up. I walked to the bathroom past the glossy blood-red walls. I painted the whole living room red at the time because I read to pick a bold color to paint your living room. Lord knows why I chose red, but I regretted it instantly. It felt like the room was trying to attack me. I later found out advertising agencies use red and yellow to attract people to food. My kitchen was yellow. No wonder I got so fat; I had a ketchup-colored living room and a mustard-colored kitchen. Yellow is my favorite color; white is also a favorite color of mine.

Those days I couldn't tell one organ or body part from another. My heart, my lungs, my stomach were all smushed together into one big blob. I walked to the bathroom to wash my face and caught myself in the mirror. *Who is that? I have no idea!* I remember wondering what my face looked like under there. I had black marks from hyperpigmentation all over my skin, caused by the food I ate, which struggled to escape through my pores and blocked the hair follicles. That, combined with my lack of discipline, touching and picking at the marks, caused me to have blemishes all over my face and body. I realize now that what I did to my skin was a form of cutting. I hacked at my face, back, and chest as a form of release. I had no idea back then; I thought I was just trying to fix my acne.

I was wearing a large robe I had bought from a vintage shop in Connecticut the weekend before. I couldn't believe I had just eaten again after the massive Korean lunch I feasted on in Palisades Park, New Jersey, with the Israeli. I met him in a halal on Bergenline Avenue in Guttenberg, New Jersey, in early 2007. Halal in Arabic means permitted, so for food, this means that the food sold there is allowed to be eaten under Islamic law. For meat, it means it has come to your plate following those laws. Different religions have laws pertaining to food. For Jewish people, it is referred to as Kosher. I was there to buy lamb, and he was behind me telling me what meat to buy. He was a very round man, and he knew his food. He was speaking to the man in Arabic and not Hebrew. It was comforting to see two people who the news would typically portray as enemies getting along quite well. I knew where they were both from because my father had been a United Nations ambassador.

I've met people from all over the world. I can quickly tell where people are from, especially if they speak their language. I love language. Even if I am not fluent in a language, I can usually understand some of it. I pick it up in their expression and movement. No language in the world sounds foreign to me, even if I don't speak it. I hear language with my entire body, not just my ears. Diplomats' daughter things—we know people, we read them quickly, and then we act appropriately in order to respect their culture.

The Israeli picked my meat, and the man wrapped it in wax paper. It was the old-fashioned way. I love to watch a butcher wrap meat in parchment. It reminds me of back home in Cameroon, where I was born, or of places in the world where meat is fresh and not much has happened to it before it arrives on your plate. He was so pleased and proud to select that lamb for me. He was such a warm soul. He invited me out to eat. He seemed to be very pleasant, so I agreed. We walked outside, and he asked me to follow him to his car so he could give me his phone number.

When we arrived at his car, it was full of so many things…. Everything looked new, but what a pile—carpets and tools, clothes and wood. Such a mess! I had no idea what his job could be. He reached into the front (it took him a while because he was very heavy) and pulled a wallet from the dashboard. I asked him how he could pay for his things when his wallet was in the car? In his thick Israeli accent, he said, "Honey, I don't carry money in my vawwwlet."

I probed, "So where is your money?"

He pulled the most massive amount of cash I've ever seen on one human being from deep within his pocket. It was all hundreds.

Then he started to pull out maybe 20 business cards from his wallet. I noticed they all had the same name, which I gathered must be his, but one card was construction, another carpet something…. I spoke again, "Wow, you're a busy man!"

He said, "Honey, I always tell people don't ask what I do, ask what do I *not* do." I laughed, and he asked me, "Do you like Korean food?"

I said, "Very much, yes."

He said, "I'm gonna take you to the best Korean place in New Jersey. It's in Palisades Park."

I said, "I would love to." It was all very friendly and lovely. I *loved* Korean food. He looked again at the cards as if trying to decide who he would present to me. Construction guy—I got the construction card.

I gave him my number also, and he called me a half-hour later. "Let's go to the Korean place tomorrow for lunch."

I said, "Sure," and we met in Palisades Park, a place I knew very well. We walked into the restaurant, and he was so loud. I remember feeling embarrassed. All of a sudden, his bubbly personality in a Korean setting seemed out of place. I remember always eating Korean food quietly when I came here. The Korean women were very happy and smiling to see him. I was a bit surprised, but they were bubblier than I had remembered. They sat us down, and he ordered almost every meat there was on the menu. *Ahh, this is why they are so smiley.* But also, he actually *was* funny with all his run-on stories.

I appreciated that he spoke so much. Although people think I'm very outgoing, I like to be quiet. I'm usually the one bringing the energy to a room. I learned how to be that way as a child. Secretly I'm shy, but with a diplomat father who spoke around the world, I acquired skills—to be able to talk and keep people engaged. It gets exhausting, so I was enjoying his yammering on. It was relaxing not needing to carry the conversation and entertain everyone. I let the *oi kimchi*, slices of cucumber and green onion in a spicy Korean pepper paste, melt on my tongue before beginning the best part—the loud crunch! Sometimes I wasn't sure if only I could hear it in my head or if the whole room could hear it as well. I missed what he was saying as I savored the taste.

He grabbed the lettuce and began to explain to me how to eat Korean food like a Korean. I had eaten Korean many times, but I didn't feel the need to tell him I already knew. He was enjoying explaining it so much. I truly believe that if someone tells you something you already know, there's no need to say, "I know." It can serve as a reminder, and it doesn't actually change the fact that you know. Lastly, they may say it in such a way that you learn a new perspective or something entirely new. Then you find out... well, in fact, you did not know.

So, when he asked, "Do you know about how to eat Korean food?" I didn't lie.

I simply said, "Why don't you teach me what you know?"

When granted permission to share what is on their mind and heart, you will see people light up in their interaction with you. Oh, there is a deep joy in letting people be heard! He began to explain to me that Korean people put the food into the lettuce and then shove the entire portion into their mouths. This much is true. He proceeded to demonstrate.

At that moment, I knew I would never eat with him in a Korean restaurant again. He filled the lettuce entirely too much. Then began the hefty job of stuffing this into his mouth while he talked, the lettuce falling apart. Talking while eating with a full mouth, no matter how delicious the food, is horrifying to me. Every bone in my entire body went cold. *This is not what Koreans do!* I had eaten with them many times; it was a mess. The rice even went in his nose. I glanced over at the Korean ladies; they were not impressed either and were equally mortified. When he finally came up for air, I whispered softly, "Bravo, Cherie, well done you."

I've never been put off Korean food ever in my life except for *that lunch*. I ate a fair amount with all he ordered, and he placed an order to go, which they made in the kitchen. I had plenty enough left over. That night, as I shoved the burger into my mouth with the leftover bulgogi, I realized I was eating just like him. We both were addicted to food; he was just honest enough to be who he was everywhere. I was politely eating in public, and then I was coming home and binging alone, sauce dripping down my face. At that moment, I was horrified the same way I had been at him, but this time with myself.

The following day came fast. I hadn't slept again. It was becoming a real issue, and the only thing I could get to make me fall asleep was a bottle of red wine. Can you imagine using wine as a sleeping pill? Sometimes it took one bottle, other times two. I would drink a bottle of white as the day ended, then wait until much later before ultimately drinking the bottle of red. I suppose I worried about drinking them back-to-back? I mean, what kind of backward healthy choice is that? *I guess it's better to put a waiting period between bottles?* I reasoned with myself. *Well done, Africa.* That's what I was doing, and soon the effect of this choice would begin causing more problems. Yet still, there I was… sleepless.

My mother told me that drinking that much wine makes you an alcoholic. She once found a bunch of bottles I hadn't thrown away under my kitchen sink. I took a quiz in a fashion magazine to find out if I was, in fact, an alcoholic. It turns out I was not a) go to rehab right away, b) a social drinker, but rather c) drinks alone and probably should slow down. Yes, I was definitely "C." Pretty accurate, I thought. But what does a magazine know?

I went to AA. *What a drama queen,* you might think. But it was more the weight of my mother's words, both in my life and influence on my choices. I found a random AA because I didn't want to meet anyone I knew. I arrived at the meeting, and everyone was going around saying hello and telling their story. One guy said he got so drunk and high that he drove his car into his sister's living room, killing her cat and almost killing his nephew as well. I was next in line.

I had heard maybe seven horror stories at this point. I told them, "My mother said that two bottles of wine a night makes you an alcoholic. Magazines say I am not but should stop drinking at home because I'm probably depressed." They all just looked at me. At that moment, I realized I wasn't an alcoholic, but I was pretty grateful for them sharing their stories. I decided I should probably head toward no more alcohol.

Mum said that the truest test of whether I was addicted or not was to attempt to stop completely. In the same breath, I started to evaluate my overall health. I stopped drinking, and when I did, my emotions bubbling up from underneath revealed everything buried below. I also dropped weight. *When did I get so lonely?* I was sad and depressed. I cried a lot after stopping the drinking. Was I drinking to fall asleep? Or was I avoiding the night and my emotions? I was *feeling* again, and I felt bad. It was like a wave that would come over me. I could see the light through the veil between air and under the water but could not catch any waves. I was just drowning in it.

I have always been very good at being alone. Even coming from a large family, I never felt part of the crowd. I felt alone, and somewhere along the road, I guess I got good at it?

I know how to busy myself with activities. I actually thought I loved that. My alone time felt sacred and good. I prided myself over others who felt the need to always have people around them to feel good. While I was always very popular with people wanting to be around me, I still boasted about being so good at being by myself—not needy. *I live alone and travel alone. I am amazing! I'm happy! I'm fantastic! I'm good.* I believed this and danced around with the false magic of being on my own. I even destroyed relationships with men, thinking they could never live up to how good it felt being on my own.

Clingy friends never made it far with me. I didn't want to go get my nails done weekly together, or did I not know how to make friends? When people met me, they wanted to be my best friend or my lover. I loved it, but then I realized I simply didn't know the road from there…. So, the lying to myself began. I began to fulfill the ultimate loner image, which would make everyone go away. I didn't need them. *What does it even look like to be close with one another?*

I had a few best friends at that time, but they were very troubled souls. Our friendships consisted of me fixing them. What a big ego I had to think the universe sent me messes to fix and that there was nothing about myself to fix! Perhaps we didn't have troubles in the same way, but I had attracted troubled souls because I was one myself. Then I suppose, if you're honest with yourself, sometimes you realize that what you told yourself to get through something isn't how you felt at all. I wasn't a loner. I was so very lonely. I wanted love. That is the truth. Being good at being alone was a cover I drew to get through how truly alone I felt for so long. Living in New York and New Jersey, everyone is so busy trying to make money and striving for success that women not wanting marriage has become a feminist statement. *Look at her! She doesn't need a man or a family. She's on her game!*

I became a man in a sense, striving to be the man I wanted to marry. It left no room for a man in my life at all, in fact.

Breaking up with people I really wanted to be with became a pattern. Never during any of that, though, did I feel like I should start drinking again. There wasn't one day I missed drinking at all. It was actually very easy for me to drop it. In many ways, I felt better, but then I had to deal with everything I was trying to drown, bubbling back up.

Being depressed is like putting too much sauce on overcooked pasta. You can't get up! Everything is just extra heavy; everything is broken down under its own weight, without flavor. I would scream silently sometimes, *"Get me out of this, God! Get me out!"* Somehow magically, between the weight of my emotions and so much clarity coming through, I was drawn into sadness. But I also came to the exciting realization that I wanted to have love in my life *and children.*

The pathway through the darkness led to the other side, where I could make decisions based on the pain. I wanted family and dinners. I wanted to homeschool my children and work from home. I wanted to live somewhere warm, close to the beach and water. I always feel good near the water.

I wanted to be able to travel home to Cameroon. I wanted my children to have the same deep love for Cameroon that I have. I wanted a kind man with kind eyes, old-fashioned and dependable. I wanted to teach African arts and craft projects to my kids and have them learn traditional African instruments in the village. Like when I was young, my mum had taken us to the village to experience these things.

I wanted them to love the taste of *bobolo* and *mintoumba*, as I do. I also wanted my children to be open to other cultures, to know foods from all over the world, and love them as I do. I wanted to travel—all of us together. I wanted to cook and have friends over for dinner, enjoying lots and lots of laughter. I began to be downright giddy just thinking of it all one afternoon. I wanted to have this dream more than being sad about being lonely. I wanted to feel good. The depression began to interrupt my dreaming about the amazing family I wanted. As my mum had taught me, I skipped straight from the problem to the solution.

I thought to myself, *Well, what do I have to do to have these children, that husband, and that life? They won't come if I am as fat as I am now!*

When I thought about the fat, terrible thoughts came to my mind. Being overweight occupies more space in your mind than your body. Even just the simple process of getting dressed requires a bouquet of thoughts. It is exhausting to have all your mind on your body—it could be doing so many other things. It could be resting, even. Yet, men were always attracted to me, even during that time. The problem was me; I was a disaster. I couldn't believe how far off course I was in my life. How could I have let this happen to me physically and emotionally? Where had I slipped away? Everything was so unhealthy! I was a broken, stumbling version of myself. Then *boom!* Back to depression. My thoughts were becoming things and feelings I didn't want.

For instance, after a day of self-loathing thoughts, I found out that I was obese one Manhattan evening. Just grab a 25-pound weight and try walking around with it all day. I was walking around with an extra 120 pounds over my normal weight of 130 pounds.

I was at Greta's house. My best friend, an Italian supermodel, was even more super on the inside than the outside. She was having some kind of friends gathering, and we ate a lot. Everyone was getting on the scale, and I was reading out their weight. *They were all so skinny!*

Then, it was my turn. I waited until all the skinny people left because I realized I hadn't weighed myself in years. I jumped off the scale like *What? I am 250. No way!* Then I jumped back on to double-check because there was no way it was right. I was *251!* Good Lord! The air I breathed in must have weighed a pound. I was shocked.

I told Greta after everyone left. She was very kind about it, and she told me to eat minestrone soup for supper. She said that she did this before she had a swimsuit or lingerie shoot. She told me that I had accomplished so much for others being an activist, and it was time to accomplish something for myself. She was right. It was definitely time for an overhaul.

I stopped thinking about how fat I was, and I started to run a fine-tooth comb through the strands of my life. Greta also suggested I go to therapy, and I trusted her, so I found a therapist.

I was reviewing my life with the therapist. She asked me all these questions: "Where were you born?" and "What was your relationship with your mother and your father?" and "Dating, what happens there?" Great questions! I was ready to do the work on myself to be well mentally, physically… all of it. It made me start to put my life into context. It made me recall so many things from childhood. I would figure out how I began and how I came to this place. Let the rewind begin!

2

In 1978, a young Korean man rode his motorcycle across Cameroon and other parts of West Africa. One afternoon, the Korean's moto broke down. Not surprising, as the roads in Edea are still rough to ride. When we go, there are some parts where we have to get out of the car and walk.

He picked up the moto and pushed it to a nearby house. He was so tired that he lay down to sleep on the veranda of the house. While waiting for the occupant to return so he could ask for help, he fell asleep. Later in the evening, a pastor came home to find the Korean sleeping at his front door. He woke the Korean, who was startled and apologetic.

The pastor and his beautiful wife, Suzanne—a thin, elegant woman wearing a scarf on her head—asked him to come in and treated him like family. She was a traditional African woman with the elegance of an off-the-set movie star and a smile to light any room. It is almost certain that she quickly put out a wooden bowl of peanuts and a bottle of palm wine or beer, water, and a napkin in their simple home. Then as she went back to the kitchen, she would be sure to begin to prepare *mintoumba*, my most favorite Cameroonian food of the Basaa people from Cameroon. I figure they had this because mintoumba is made in bulk and then reheated as a snack that is a mini-meal in itself. You can easily get full from eating mintoumba, so I am sure she would have quickly grabbed a loaf, cut it into slices, and reheated it in the crunch of an unexpected stranger.

Mintoumba is fermented cassava (manioc). You mix manioc, red palm oil, water, *piment* (pepper in French), and salt to make a doughy, savory cake. You peel the brown skin off of the manioc, which looks like a hard brown branch. The outside is brown and rough; the inside of it is white. You cut the manioc into small pieces and leave it to soak for a few days. You can also add a little salt to the soaking process. On the fourth day, you remove the manioc, rinse it well, and remove the root strings. Following this, you squeeze the excess water, and you will find it feels like the beginnings of a good dough for dumplings, except wetter. Once the water has been removed, it is pounded, then seasoned with red palm oil and other seasonings. The dough looks egg yolk-yellow. Wrap the dough in a banana leaf. Then fold the leaf to cover the dough like an envelope and tie it with string. Steam the banana leaf-wrapped dough. It makes a soft, slightly spicy yellow cake, similar in consistency to Korean rice cakes called *tteok*. This cake can be sliced and grilled on an open fire. It makes for a slightly crispy on the outside while soft and moist on the inside bite. It's near close to heaven on Earth in your mouth.

Basaa women make it in bulk. It is frozen and much like in Korean culture where a mother might steam homemade *mandu* (dumplings), the same with Cameroonian-Basaa women, except instead of mandu, it's mintoumba. She *must* have given him mintoumba. She must have served him plantain and another cassava-based side called *bobolo*, a long white sausage-like tube encased in a leaf bound with string. He would have been the recipient of a feast prepared quickly, but that took many, many weeks to harvest and prepare in advance. Slow, fast food—the mistaken simple elegance and ease of a traditional African woman—takes a lot of hard work.

The next day, the pastor's daughter came to visit her parents. Her name was Ruth. She was pregnant with her second child. She was fascinated with how this had all come to pass. She and the Korean took a photograph together.

The pastor was my grandfather, Pastor Joseph Tjega. Soon after that chance meeting, he died. I was born that November to Ruth. My mother gave birth to me at the time of year when on the other side of the world, Korean women perform a process called *kimjang*, where they prepare kimchi for their families in large amounts. Women of the same family gather together, rubbing a red pepper powder-based paste mixed with chopped raw vegetables onto salted cabbage leaves and radish, which they wrap and ferment to make the most famous Korean side dish in cuisine: *kimchi*.

Baechu (cabbage) kimchi, the most recognizable of all the kimchi, is rich in vitamins A, K, folate, potassium, choline, beta carotene, calcium, pre and probiotics, and more. This napa cabbage side dish consists of garlic, ginger, Asian pear, onion, fish sauce, salted shrimp, green onions, white onions, hot pepper flakes, sweet rice flour, and carrots. Different regions of

Korea swap the salted shrimp for squid, oysters, or other salty substitutes.

In the first step, the cabbage is hand-torn into quarters. It is then salted, soaked, turned periodically, then rinsed and drip-dried. At this time, porridge is made of sweet rice flour known as *chapssal garu* and water; some add sugar to this porridge. While the porridge is cooling, mince and blend the Asian pear, garlic, ginger, and onion. This mixture, along with fish sauce and hot pepper flakes, known as *gochugaru,* is mixed into the now cooled porridge.

Next, the salted shrimp, or whatever chosen salted seafood, is added to the now peppery paste, leaving you two steps away from the end of this magic recipe. Chop green onions, julienne radish and carrots, and some add chopped leek or *minari* (water dropwort). Add all this raw to the peppery paste and mix. Now you have your kimchi paste. You return to the napa cabbage and apply the paste between the leaves and cover them completely before rolling them up and putting them into a container called an *onngi*. In modern times, any airtight container can be used.

One can eat it straight away, and this is called fresh kimchi, but most leave the container of kimchi outside the fridge for four days to ferment before transferring it to the refrigerator. In the olden days, it was buried in the ground in an onngi, which is still done in Korea in rural areas. It is crunchy, spicy, and juicy. Kimchi is an electric living food!

This kimchi, which they make together during Kimjang in November, is shared among the family and lasts through winter.

So, maybe the Korean knew, because of his mother, how much work that my grandmother put into his meal? He was probably respectful because this tale is one I was told over and over. Because of this, I have had a fondness for Koreans since I was a small child. But of course, there is more to me than my maternal grandparents.

The therapist asked me so many questions about my father. I suppose if a girl is having troubles in the love department, they ask about her father? I leaned into her beautiful sofa but didn't want to lay down, as I wore too much makeup those days to cover my blemishes. It was our second session. She had asked me last session to draw a picture of my parents' faces as a mask and draw their story behind them. My godfather had come to Manhattan to see me during the week, so I had peppered him with a million questions about my father and mother and everything he could remember. With that information and what I knew, I drew my father's face. It was an ocean of water, and at the bottom of that ocean, there was a boy. He was crying beside a grave. My paternal grandmother died when my father was a boy. I don't think he ever got over it, and it explained how my father could be a world-class diplomat, a most impressive lion of a man, and a small little boy, simultaneously. I continued that pattern in my own life, and it took a long time for me to recognize the blessing that duality gave me, as well as the problems it caused. His grandfather, my paternal great-grandfather, had two (maybe more?) wives. In Cameroon at the time, this was perfectly normal. That means that on my father's side, there are two separate families.

Speaking of carrying on patterns, my father didn't marry two women at the same time, but he did continue this pattern. The concept of one or two, sometimes three, families continued. My father has given me the wonderful gift of seven siblings. Since my father had different women mothering his children, by nature, this caused some jealousy because it's only natural for children to want their father's attention. By the time I came along, all of my siblings, minus my full brother, Bamela, were much older. Bam is only two years older. Some were 20 years my senior. So, my need for attention came from the fact that I was two years old, and their need for attention came from the fact they probably had not received enough attention since they were two years old. That's my perception. I could not tell you their entire journey. I don't know because we are not close enough to speak that way. At any rate, so continued a fierce battle for who mattered most with absolutely no one as the winner.

When I was little, I wanted so much to be close to my siblings, but that warm, safe feeling just never happened. I suppose this is where my loneliness began, because I really loved them all so much. I remember wanting hugs and fun but not getting it from most of my siblings. Sometimes we had fun, but many mean words were also said to me behind our parents' backs. I am close with two of my siblings: my sister Babs and my brother Bamela. However, I genuinely am in love with all my siblings, for better or worse. The moments I get to be close with any of them, even for a little while, I treasure with all my heart.

I was a little girl in a big family but felt all by myself. I used to go to my room and pretend a lot. I used to have my dolls for company. I would throw grand parties—dinner parties with all my dolls and imaginary people from the American movies my father would make us watch. I believe my love for American cinema and entertainment began right then. I served presidents and movie stars at those dinner parties, and I cooked everything myself. "Bonjour Monsieur le Président, would you like to sit with Madeleine, my doll, or Marilyn Monroe? Oh yes, of course, Marilyn, you want more *bongo chobi*? Have some bobolo and tea. A big fish has been prepared for you." All my pretend play included me preparing the food, don't you know? We had to have *all* the foods.

My mother's side of the family—a warm, friendly, and especially loving group of siblings—was the best thing about my life in Cameroon. We would have large dinners as a family once a month, so I knew just what to do. My late aunt Lydia was so tender with me. She would always touch my face and smile, looking directly into my eyes. She was in charge of food, so if I learned to be responsible for food and dinner parties anywhere, it was from her.

My mother was not much about cooking, but her skill for decorating a room is legendary. She knows how to pick the perfect flowers and make modern African designs to magazine levels. My Aunt Teclaire, Ton Ton Paul, Uncle Simon, Tatas Lea and Louise, and Tata Pauline loved me so hard. The warmth of Pastor Tjega's family is the reason I exist and never fall all the way off course. When we left them in Cameroon, that family feeling became a hole I could never fill again. I missed them so much! I can't even tell you how much; I cried about it a lot. My cousin James was so loving; I always remember him and his big smile. When we moved to New York after my father was appointed Ambassador to the United Nations the first time, they were all suddenly gone and missing from my life. I loved New York, but with no family at all anymore, I was gutted and just six years old.

"Get back to your father," the therapist instructed, keeping me on track when I would go off-topic. "What is his crying near a grave doing to you?"

"I believe that because he was grieving his mum, he never quite let women get very close to him—to hurt him that way again," I said.

"Even you?" she asked.

"Yes, even me."

"My father was a great man," I told her, "and we were close in some ways for one reason." She probed for more, and I continued, "I figured out what my father loved and was passionate about, and I connected with him on those points. We got to have a wonderful relationship, and he wasn't void of love. In fact, because of the ever-present little boy he was, he was the most outwardly loving man you ever met. So sweet and extremely romantic, full of life and joy."

"Then he did love you?"

"Absolutely," I told her. "A mad passionate all-consuming type of love that was extremely missed when he wasn't there." No one could make me feel so loved and *seen* as my father when he was there. When he wasn't there for such long periods of time, it hurt me so much. I missed him. Oh, did I miss him and his funny games and dances. He was so fun! Everyone loved him— you couldn't *not*. Imagine meeting the biggest movie star in the world, and then they are so friendly—not acting Hollywood or mean or rude—kind and caring, worldly, full of experiences and stories. Lovely. Who wouldn't miss that?

She asked, "Where was he?"

He was working—not ridiculous money-seeking work, but world-changing work, honorable and good work—as a diplomat. His integrity, mixed with his deep understanding of international law, made him a giant. I don't think of my father as working so much as I think he was *needed*, because of what a brilliant man he was. He was passionate about his work, but his true love was his country, Cameroon. He loved to be there and advocate for his people and African people in general.

"Tell me more about him," she prodded.

Paul Bamela Engo was born in Ebolowa, Cameroon, on October 21, 1931. He lived most of his early life in Nigeria, where he attended Edo College in Benin. After graduating, he went to London, England, where he studied law at Middle

Temple Inn. That's how he became a lawyer, and he went on to become an International Court Judge. But also, in all of his outstanding achievements, his proudest honor was to twice be the Ambassador to the United Nations for Cameroon in New York.

"But there was something else special about my dad," I continued. While he was in London, he was affiliated with the London Amateur Athletic Club. He was a triple-jumper. His athletic ability took him to the 1956 Summer Olympics, where he represented Nigeria in Melbourne. He was a man who didn't half-heartedly do things. Mediocrity was not in his system. In almost everything he did, he excelled. To have something in common with him, I attached myself to the key things in his life. My father and I always had loads to talk about when he was around. He was an athlete, so I became one and competed. He even once came when I was running track in high school in 1993. He sat on the bus that left my high school in New Jersey. The track coach told my father that no parents were allowed on the bus.

He asked the coach, "Who is the finest athlete on your team?" The coach said it was me. Then he asked the coach, "Do you think that mental preparation is important for an athlete's performance at a state competition?" My coach said yes. He then asked the coach, "If you could have an Olympic athlete speak with that athlete to give them performance insight or motivation on the way to the meet, would you?"

Of course, the coach agreed, and my father said, "Then, today is your lucky day." He walked onto the bus with his *agbada*, the traditional clothing of men of Cameroon and Nigeria. The coach then announced that my father would speak to them on the way to the meet. My father looked shocked to me but calm to everyone else. He never said he wanted to talk to *all the bus*. He spoke loudly, "You are all wonderful athletes! Remember, though, this is a race, and the person who wins is the winner." This was his shortest speech in the history of him speaking around the world.

I was dying with laughter on the inside! He gathered together his agbada and sat down. The bus seat was small, and the material of his full agbada took up lots of room. It created a closeness between him, me, and all the fabric. It was a blueish-grey with gold embroidery. I felt it on my face and leaned into him. I loved him so much! I could have stayed there forever in his agbada, so close, feeling the deep vibration of his voice that made him a world-class speaker, along with his mastery of the English language. With his poetic voice, strong intonation, and overall grace, he was an excellent orator and seemed so wonderful to me. He began to talk to me about performance, starts, and the mentality of winning a race; this went on for the entire ride. I never felt so loved. He chose to give all of his attention to me that day. It was so magical. When we got to the meet, he showed me a good angle to pounce out at the start. That little tip, plus all the talk he gave me on the bus... I WON!

He was so good at being a father—*Wow, encore! Encore! More, MORE!*—I craved it.

So, it seems I had not drawn my father in an ocean mourning his mother, who he lost. I had drawn me, missing that part of our relationship. The therapy was good for me. It made me feel lighter every time I left, as if a weight was being lifted from me.

She asked me about my mother next, and this time she asked how my mother was significant to who I was.

Well, with my mother, things were so much easier to explain. She is the very reason I hold my head high, because her love—while not always affectionate and lovey-dovey—was ever-present. My mother doesn't even have to be in the room to mother me. My life would be a completely different story were it not for what my mother did to mold me in the first ten years of my life. But this is a love story, and my deep capacity for self-love and why I could not stay drowned was because my mother not only made me know that anything I can dream is possible, but she also taught me how to manifest things in my life. She did that by providing a sense of security that she would be there for me no matter what I did or what choices I made. I think she is the only person I have met that has shown me true unconditional love. She never abandons me *EVER*, even when she doesn't like me very much. That kind of loyalty stays with you forever. It doesn't mean we had a perfect relationship, but we never broke away from each other. We always went through things together. My queen of a mother, Ruth Engo, née Ngo Tjega, is the greatest woman alive. She not only supported my father in everything he did but made paths of her own. She served in the Office of the Special Adviser on Africa to the Secretary-General of the United Nations, Kofi Annan. She also founded and continues to serve as the president for African Action on AIDS, a charity whose chief concern is African girls and sanitation in Sub-Saharan Africa. My mother is an accomplished woman. When my father became an ambassador to the United Nations, she gave that up and stayed home with us in New York. Then she slowly rebuilt her career after taking time to go to every single game, concert, swim meet, doctor's appointment, and hear every song or poem I wrote. She created global opportunities for my poetry to be heard; she was my first talent manager. Even long after going back to work, she still miraculously made me feel seen and heard.

I looked up to both my parents all my life and still do. Because of this, I wanted to be with them in their global work and became a child activist at a very early age. I spoke to the United Nations in 1984 in the General Assembly for the first time. I was only six. I remember that morning well. I climbed into the car, my heart pounding and my thoughts scattered as the car drove through the city streets of New York. Each turn brought us ever closer to our destination: an enormous, important place only a few kids in the world like me knew well.

When the car finally stopped, I looked around the back seat to make sure I didn't leave anything. Mum, who had gone earlier than us, was now at the window talking to our driver. She motioned for me to open my door. Mum never let our drivers open the door for us, thinking it would spoil us. I saw her big, beautiful smile as the air hit my face. "Did you prepare on the drive?" she asked.

"Yes, Mum, I did." I would do anything to make Mum proud. She reminded me that I could do this. There wasn't anything I couldn't handle. I stepped out of the car and looked up at this five-hundred-foot-tall building the whole world knew as the United Nations. I knew it as the place where my father worked. But this wasn't *Bring Your Children to Work Day*, this was *World Children's Day*, and I was expected to speak.

I straightened out my *kaba* and put one foot in front of the other. I walked through the front doors and was directed to the General Assembly room, where I immediately saw children from all over the world. We were all dressed in the traditional garments of our homelands. Most of the other kids were much older than I. I was shown to my father's official seat. I watched as announcements were made, awards were given, and *World Children's Day 1984* activities were put into motion. Then, my turn came. There was a camera from the American Broadcasting Company filming me.

"The speaker from Cameroon has the floor," the chairman said. I took a deep breath, leaned forward to the microphone, and made my first of many speeches at the United Nations.

I had dreams of helping people in my life, and I wanted it to start right then. I believed children had the greatest possibility for change. When you address a global audience, there is a pause between the beginning of the performance of a speech where you literally could either fall into a dark hole or soar to the sky. In that pause, you either fold to fear or take all the elements that fear creates in your body chemistry, and you can change lives with it. Then there is another pause as you land before the applause. The *applause pause* scares me much more than the first. It's the moment where you see if what you said landed in such a way that you can use it to work in the future. "You're only as good as your last picture," is a Hollywood saying. The same goes for speeches. Even if you do great work, support comes from connecting what you do to making people feel who they are in that moment is meant to be part of changing the issue. I have been very aware of the pauses and performances in life that followed me since that speech. When everyone applauded my speech, I realized I could accomplish great things with my life, and there was no reason I had to wait. As I sat in my father's chair, I realized something else. It was a humbling experience, and I had a lot to prove.

The therapist asked, "Did this bring pressure to your life?"
"No."
I told her that I loved being in global affairs and that whole world of helping people. I was fortunate to grow up in the diplomatic world and see people trying to change the world. As the daughter of a United Nations ambassador, I met great people and did many wondrous things that put a magical

context to my life. Most of them still have an influence on me to this day. Meeting Arthur Ashe, seeing world leaders speak, meeting celebrities who cared about causes… made me believe that world-changers and celebrities were the same.

One evening that remains with me—I was probably 17 or so—was when I met Harry Belafonte at the United Nations. It was at a reception after former South African President Nelson Mandela spoke on the lawn after a beautiful concert in his honor. My mum had a friend by the name of Hugh Locke, a world-class philanthropist and event planner. He organized the entire event and concert that followed.

At the reception, Mr. Belafonte and I both reached for an hors d'oeuvres at the same time. Of course, my first reaction was, "Whoa. Harry Belafonte." I meant to say it in my head, but it came out of my mouth. I am not one to be starstruck at all, but it was Harry Belafonte. Come on.

I remember him laughing, and for some reason, I noticed his perfect teeth. It was like the sun shined from his face. I mean, if you ever had the luck to see that smile close up, you're a lucky person.

I had better training than that, though. It was an awkward moment. I immediately thought I better ask him something. My father told me if you're ever in doubt in a social situation, the best thing to do every time is to ask a question. It's a great way to recover, and there are several reasons why. First, it turns the situation around, and suddenly, it's not about you. Second, you may learn something new, which is always good.

So, I asked, "Why should people give?"

He looked at me with a gentle nod. "Because they noticed."

That was interesting. I followed up. "What does that mean?"

"If you notice injustice," he started, "or if you notice pain or you notice a need someone has that could make their life better, you should do something. Giving is doing something. They don't need to look like you or be from your neighborhood or even be your same race. If you notice, you shouldn't let it slide. There's a reason you noticed, and that's because there's something in you. There's something about you that can make a change in that situation, or you wouldn't have noticed."

That's what it was like to grow up around the United Nations. I never knew who I would bump into or who I would end up getting into a conversation with. Great things happened all the time, and they had a huge impact on my life. Those words Harry Belafonte spoke to me that day followed me throughout my life. I live my life by that, and my life has been better for it. It was not just meeting celebrities but hearing cases and stories of people's triumph through misfortune. There are so many tales of adversity, enough to leave gratitude running through my veins for a lifetime.

After therapy one day, I remember going to my car and the light shining into my vehicle. I was on River Road in Edgewater,

New Jersey, where my therapist lived by the water. I lived very close in Guttenberg, New Jersey, at the time. The sun was beating down on my face, and I felt so good. The depression was lifting. I was telling stories, and things were just shifting into place. I must have been about 28 years old. My activism took me on many adventures. At that time, I blended my passion for entertainment with my calling to serve in the fight against AIDS. I ran a film festival partnering with the United Nations, MTV, and New York University called *The New York AIDS Film Festival.*

I was also promoting Hollywood films with social messages. The Senior Vice President of Strategic Partnerships & Public Affairs at MTV, Ian Rowe—a man who showed me what it looks like when someone supports young people's visions—introduced me to an American cinema house. That led me to start film promotion, and I continued partnering with TV networks to promote AIDS education content. It was all good work, and I was running a few charitable initiatives as well, but it left little time for life. I suppose I understood the busy ways of my parents more? Changing the world and travel does not always leave much room for a family because changing the world is never-ending. There's no clocking out for famine, AIDS, poverty, orphans, etc.

I was unhappily single, fat, lonely, and extremely popular— *huzzah!* But being a popular woman with a great phone book of American entertainment personalities, activists, and international diplomats, reminiscent of my childhood parties, did nothing for my personal growth. All the best dinner parties I did throw or attend simply did not take the loneliness away.

Manhattan is actually full of popular lonely people like me. Some of the loneliest were also the most famous. I have wiped the lonely tears of a movie star/supermodel or two after a dinner or charity gala. Some I didn't know well and had met only that night; some I knew quite well. Popularity should be listed as a symptom of loneliness if you ask me.

As the sun hit me that day, I was sitting there feeling so hopeful about life. I could feel my grandmother around me like a circle of light. I had been telling my mother, who now was living back in Cameroon after retiring from the United Nations, that I wished I had known my grandmother, who died after I was born. I was too little to remember life with her, though she adored me; this I knew. I could just feel her, and I could not place how or why. I just could.

We ended up in New Jersey when my father decided he would leave the UN and go back to Cameroon. My mum decided to stay, not wanting to uproot us again. He thought it would be best to get two of my many sisters an apartment in New York City. They were in their early twenties at the time. So, he asked his secretary to find one, but she wasn't familiar with the nicer, safer areas of New York. I don't say that with any disrespect, but rather to express that, in general, immigrants tend to live in certain places in the city. There is a comfort to a neighborhood where you can find other people from your home country. Many Africans I know haven't left the Bronx to move to places like Manhattan. There's a sort of segregation still quite alive in New York and New Jersey, both widely known for their diversity.

New York is quite segregated. I have been to many events where it was white-only with an all-black serving crew, which made me so uncomfortable. I remember going to a media luncheon in Manhattan once. The server addressed me and said, "Yessum," and I almost passed out. We were not billionaires, but I was exposed to very wealthy circles due to my father's position.

For a long time, I would have to pilgrimage to other boroughs to get ethnic products for my hair and skin. I loved Harlem so much. Of the many places I have lived in the world, I wish I would have lived there, too. Many a time, I had to find Africans to get some fresh shea butter or black soap. It actually is all segregated—although no one likes to talk about it.

The Africans could be found in the Bronx and parts of Queens, Russian Jews in Brooklyn, Koreans in Queens and New Jersey, white people in Manhattan…. Of course, there are always exceptions; I was one of them. I am just describing what I observed and experienced. I once took a cab when I was living in Manhattan. The cab driver said to me, "You live in Manhattan?" I think there's a pot, but I would not quite describe it as *melted*. It's more like there are many different vegetables, and they don't always make the tastiest soup.

My mother stayed on at the UN. My father went back to Cameroon and split his time in Hamburg, Germany, when he was elected an International Court Judge. He presided as one of two African judges on the International Tribunal for the Law of the Sea. They continued their marriage, but not on the same continent.

"How did that manifest itself in your relationships?" the therapist once asked me. I explained to her that long-distance became a prerequisite for some of my favorite boyfriends. If they lived downtown, a cab ride away, no thanks!

Oh, you live in Australia, you say? Fantastic! I love you. At any rate, when my mother heard my two sisters' apartment was in an unsafe neighborhood, she went to live with them. I was 11 and attending a boarding school in England. When I came home for break, this apartment was a very new experience as the area was unsafe.

All my life, I had been used to walking up the street and visiting friends, playing outside, and being free. But when I came to stay in this apartment, I couldn't go anywhere. I wasn't allowed to roam as I pleased. Mum tried to keep me busy enough, but it was a massive change from the way things used to be. Getting used to it was hard.

I remember wanting to go back to boarding school in Kent, England, so bad. Usually, I couldn't wait to get home from boarding school. But I think this experience made me quite fond of England.

While I was back in England, my mum had a colleague in New Jersey who knew where a spacious and safe apartment was with two pools, an inside and an outside one. There was a tennis court and a basketball court. It was called *The Galaxy*. I mean, it even had a movie theatre. On the summer holiday, when I came back and saw the place, I sighed with relief as the burden was lifted. That's how we left New York for New Jersey.

3

At one point, I left England and attended boarding school for the first time in New York. Then I switched and went to a high school in the small town of Leonia, New Jersey. (That's where I was on the track team when my father came to the meet.) Bye-bye, Yorkshire pudding, tea, and crumpets. Hello Taylor Ham, egg and cheese, and kimchi! Leonia is the neighboring town of a city full of Korean families, Korean bakeries, Korean shops, and Korean signs written in *Hangul.*

Hangul is the Korean alphabet invented by King Sejong the Great, the fourth king of the Joseon Dynasty. The language first went by *Hunminjeongeum,* which means "the right sounds to be taught to the people." Hangul is a great source of pride for Korean people.

These "right sounds" I heard spoken among the beautiful people of Pal Park. In the Korean language known as *Hangukeo,* Hangul is the writing, and Hangukeo is the spoken language. I've learned over the years that Palisades Park, New Jersey, has the highest concentration of Koreans in the country. California has more Koreans by far, but they are more spread out.

Most Korean kids I knew spoke Korean, as did their parents. They were born in Korea and had come here when they were young, so they also spoke perfect English. In that sense, they were like me.

I came to America from Cameroon very young, so now I can relate as African American but firmly maintain my African identity. African with America and a side of England. My name was Suzanne—nicknamed Africa—but named after my grandmother Suzanne. People called me "Suzy Africa."

We were the same in that way, caught in two places, yet fitting nowhere. They were American kids as much as America would let them be American, with this solid Korean base at home. When I visited their homes in Pal Park, I felt like I was in Little Korea. They had pretty folding panels and beautiful brass plates that made me love the elegant Korean vibe. The pots were different, and the smells were different. Yummy smells! I love the smells of Korean food. I first ate kimchi when I was at the United Nations School in Manhattan at age six, and I loved it!

One thing, though. Their parents spoke Korean with them at home while encouraging their kids to become more American. In their house, they spoke Korean like Mum spoke French to me. Some of their grandmothers didn't speak English at all. That was the way it was for kids born in Korea. Then, Korean American kids born in America spoke mixed Korean and English to their parents at home but spoke English outside. Though as the years went by, it would be more and more English. I wish I had kept in touch with some of them. I am such a move-on kind of girl, but I did continue to frequent the town of Palisades Park.

I was going to school, and I had Korean friends—not best friends, but I knew Korean kids. Now looking back, some Korean vibration was ever-present in my life. Even the apartment Mum bought, she bought from Koreans. I continued to have Korean friends in my life in Manhattan and New Jersey. I could make friends easily because I have a big mouth. At a bus stop or a grocery, I connect with people with ease.

As I was graduating from NYU, I met a girl. She was a designer with a small shop in SoHo. She grew up in Pal Park, and she took me to a Korean spa. I was the only black person there. Now there are people of all races who go there, but back then, at King Sauna, I was the only non-Korean there.

We ate *patbingsu* in the spa. Patbingsu is a Korean dessert of powdery delicate shaved ice in a cup, with condensed milk poured over it, topped with sweet red beans, fruits, and whatever you like—even brownies in some cases. Topping choices can seem endless. At the spa, they only offered ice, beans, and fruit. I don't have a sweet tooth, so the bean paste was too sugary for me. I would have it with just the milk, or more often than not, just the ice and fruits. It is incredibly refreshing when you come out of the steam or sauna, sweating and so hot. These tiny drops of creamy ice flakes melt on your tongue, and the cold races the milk to envelop your mouth, throat, and belly. *It's so yummy!*

I am African, so eating ice and fruits to cool down is perfectly normal to me. But sweet beans were something I didn't learn to appreciate until much later. It was very different for me because, for a West African, beans are always eaten hot and savory. But I always ordered it and ate around it so as not to offend anyone.

Being the only black girl didn't seem to matter, or maybe it did, but no one told me. I was so skinny in those days, also comfortable naked, thanks to my mum who took me to many spas. She had explained the history behind the shape of my breasts and told me they looked like the breasts of women in my tribe. I could never be uncomfortable or compare myself with other women's bodies. I find myself beautiful because I know the story of my body parts. My nose and my beautiful brown skin make me very special—I was told this. That helps a lot to *want* to be black. For most of my life, I wanted darker skin because Mum painted black as beautiful.

I also was used to being the only black person somewhere. I got looks, but everyone was always friendly to me. Otherwise, I would have never returned. The Korean spa, or *jjimjilbang*, is a public bathhouse. They have steam rooms, hot stone rooms, saunas, scrub massages, food, and spaces to sleep. They are open 24 hours a day. You pay an entry fee of about 40 dollars, and then whatever else you do there is added to your tab. You pay for all of it at the door when you leave. You leave your car key, and then once you pay, you get it back.

As you enter the locker room, you are given a pair of shorts and a t-shirt, which are mandatory for everyone to wear. You must first shower and wash your hair. Then you can make an appointment for a scrub and massage. In the meantime, you wander around and pamper yourself. You can go in a hot tub or an ice-cold pool. You can lay in a room on hot stones and sleep. You can also schedule other things like a hair appointment, a manicure or pedicure, acupuncture… it's endless! For another 40 dollars, you can even sleep there. I once met a woman who came there from another state and stayed there a week.

When you go to a Western spa, you can't have a full-on feast. They only serve you one olive on a single crisp with a lettuce leaf. When you go to a Korean spa, you can eat like a king: *bibimbap* (a mixed rice and vegetable bowl), a big bowl of soup, and *banchan* side dishes are refilled upon request. The essentials of Korean cuisine are on the menu. Afterward, you can go lay down. I never ate a full meal there until many years later. Mostly I ate shaved ice with fruits and slightly brownish Korean baked eggs called *maekbanseok gyeran* that are stone-baked for three hours. I drank fresh fruit juices and lots of water.

Once your appointment time comes, you are asked to sit in the steam room first. Then the magic begins. An older woman in black underwear uses all her sheer force to scrub any dead skin off your body with a small scrub sponge. The first time I had it done, I was horrified. I couldn't believe how much skin came off! I thought they scrubbed the black off me. *Bloody hell, have I not been cleaning my skin properly?*

It feels amazing. You are tossed around like a rag doll, and every inch of you is sloughed off. Once finished, they wash you off with a bucket of warm to hot water—a moment that is almost holy as all of the dead skin cells are washed away. You emerge a new person! Then they massage you, walk on your back, and place refreshingly cold cucumber slices on your face. The best part…? *You don't have to leave!* I love going to spas, but the worst thing is having a great treatment and being rushed back to the chaos of the street, especially in Manhattan. It's harsh!

In the Korean jjimjilbang, you can lay on a floor of hot stones or an oversized reclining massage chair and sleep for five hours. Talk about the deep restoration of your body and mind! There is nothing more rejuvenating to me than a jjimjilbang day or two in a row.

The sauna and food areas are where you wear the pink shirt and shorts they give you at the door. Men wear blue shorts and shirts. In these areas, men and women can mix and mingle. But where there are steam, hot tubs, and massages, men and women are separated, so you are free to walk around naked. From birth to age 20, I had regular exposure to Korean culture, whether it was a meal at a Korean barbecue after school, a spa experience, my mother's Korean friends, and more. It was an ever-present reality in my life. I didn't think much of it. Unaware, this underlying theme kept nudging me along.

4

So that day after my therapy session in Edgewater, I was in my car, sun glowing on my face. The weight of depression was lifting, and I felt my grandma Suzanne's loving energy and presence. I decided to go for a drive, as we did when I was younger. With just music playing and driving, I ended up back in Palisades Park, and all these memories flooded my mind.

When my mum was a little unwell and still living in the States, her Korean friend introduced her to a shop in a strip mall. We started going there every Sunday after church. They had heated stone beds with soft lights in the rooms and a relaxing atmosphere. People were coming to this store for healing. I had never been to a place where they let you use the equipment for healing that was actually for sale.

Koreans take care of each other in that sense. The businesses look out for each other. They might come across as harsh, but they take care of each other when it comes to their community. If more stores worked that way and let people use the healing equipment, they'd probably sell way more stuff.

As I was driving, I remembered this and turned into that mall area and walked inside to find it had moved locations. I asked around to see where it might have moved, and I stumbled onto a woman who was selling delicious Korean bread. It was freshly baked with a buttery cream inside of it. Just smelling it was enough to make my mouth water.

A major difference about Korean grocery stores back then was that they make you taste stuff. *Everywhere* you go in the store, they have samples, and you get to taste them before you buy them. *Fat girl heaven!* So, this lady was outside with this Korean bread, and she gave me a sample. I couldn't believe how good it was; melted cream and bread on my tongue, on my cheek, in my teeth, the smell… the leftovers on my fingers.

As she looked at me, she said in her Korean accent, "Two for seven. This *ppang* is three for ten."

I asked for six bags. As the lady started loading up my order, a voice came out of nowhere: "You are too fat-uh."

That caught me strange. I cocked my head. *What?* I couldn't believe it. Did someone straight-up just call me fat? A harsh dose of reality after feeling so good that day. The depression lifted the emotional weight, but it didn't burn my fat quite as fast. Here was the reality of that in my face. I could feel the temperature of my blood change, and it made my feet feel wobbly and my heart race.

Korean women are super blunt. The older ladies in Korea are called *ajumma,* while the grandmothers are called *halmoni.* When I turned around to see who had just called me fat, there was this Korean halmoni, a beautiful grandmother hurling her words at me like shoveled snow. "You are too fattuh!" If it wasn't an insult, her voice was almost pleasant-sounding—firm yet beautiful, like Korean pansori music. "You ahhh too fatuuuuh."

She was telling me directly that I shouldn't be eating that bread at my size. Her English was not that great, but she was super clear in those words.

It was all harsh reality—zero compliments. Korean moms do not play, and they aren't shy either. They tell you exactly what they are thinking. In that way, they are actually like African parents.

When I visited Cameroon, elders would take one look at me and say, "What happened to you? You are so fat. You used to be so slim." All this before they even said hello or greeted me. Once I went to my cousin's place, my little cousins were yelling, "*Gaaah voilà la plus belle femme du monde.*... You are the most beautiful woman on the planet, but you are so fat you cover it. Do sport, you will see!" They kept on for about an hour. I felt so loved and ridiculed at the same time. So, those experiences prepared me to be around older Koreans and laugh off what might upset someone else. Not this time, though. It wasn't funny, and it was public!

When I turned around to see the elderly lady who had just called me fat, I immediately recognized her age, which means respectful-African-child mode kicked in. There was no way I would tell her to shut up or ask her, "Who the hell are you?" I had to respect her because of her age. In African cultures, you have to respect your elders, period. They are elders; you show respect. That's just how it goes.

Korean culture is the same. It's like calling an older sister *unni* if you're a girl. There's a different word if you're a boy, and that's *noona*. To be polite, if you want to call an older woman unni, as in big sister, you have to ask her first politely. So, there I was with my hurt pride, not laughing it off, holding my buttercream ppang, and trying to get my dignity back. Then she started talking to the other lady as she grabbed my bread out of my hand and gave it back to her. "Why are you selling her this bread?"

The seller lady treated her with respect, but she kept trying to give me the bread back. I was standing there watching, thinking, *Damn!*

I didn't try to get my money back because I felt bad for the seller. This elderly lady just didn't care about any of us.

The seller lady gestured for me to stay. Perhaps I could come back and get the bread after the rude woman left?

This old lady was just too much. She was extra harsh about the whole thing. But for some reason, I could tell buried deep down within her was this heart which, although rough, felt almost like family trying to protect me. Afterward, I could discern the insult and actions could only be those of someone who *knew* you well. It is the same in African culture. Even when they sound unkind, there is truth in it. Even with my mum, she wasn't hurtful, but she would tell me to be careful with my health. She would warn me that I wasn't going down a good lane. Mum has *nunchi*. Nunchi is a Korean term that describes emotional intelligence and the ability to read how someone is feeling, recognize it, read the room, and then act accordingly. She has always been able to read when I am hurt. Even with her traditional way, I have never felt in my whole life that my mother was ignoring how I felt. I am very grateful for that peaceful securing love.

A woman I once knew, Kacy Duke—a celebrity trainer who trained Greta—stopped one time and looked at me like, *Whoa! What's up? I don't know what you're doing, girl, but time to stop doing it.* I immediately bought her book and left it in my fridge to remind myself to stay healthy.

Back in those days, I got a lot of questions about my weight gain. *What's happening with your weight?* Even from some people who should have been minding their own weight. I got used to them commenting, even the ones with no nunchi. But this elderly Korean lady took the cake of the *what's-happening-with-your-weight* questions. I mean, she grabbed the bag of bread and gave it back to the sales lady—no shame at all!

Somewhere in there, I felt love even though I was not sure why. Even though I felt like she had just straight-up dissed me, in a weird way, it felt like she was one of my strange family members who didn't know the polite way to say and do things. The most familiar stranger I ever encountered. I recognized there was something genuine about her, but then she started walking away.

I stopped her, and I have to admit, I had tears in my eyes, but I asked, "Okay, what should I eat then? What do you think I should eat? If you know everything about what I'm supposed to eat and everything I'm eating is bad, what do you think I should eat?"

She looked at me, and in all seriousness, she answered, "Korean food. Korean food is bestuh."

We were standing outside of this place called Han Ah Reum, which in Korean means "one arm full of groceries." Now they're called H Mart, and they're all over America in many states, and they even have stores in Canada and the UK. Food from Korean brands filled the rows, and there was a large produce section with many Korean fruits and vegetables, all designed to help Koreans keep their culture. The elderly lady gestured, and she led me into this Korean grocery store. She grabbed a cart and pointed out so much food.

I never in my life bought so many vegetables and fruits during one trip before. I nervously asked if she came all the time. I felt vulnerable and out there. "Can I see you again, here?" The words tumbled out of my mouth.

"After churchy Sunday." She turned and walked away.

"Excuse me!" She turned, and I managed, "Thank you."

She grunted and grumbled something in Korean and continued out the hallway. I looked down at my cart. I was excited to have had such a different shopping experience. I had a forest in my cart, enough to feed a thousand rabbits. Even now, that's how I shop to this day. I need two refrigerators when I come home from the grocery store.

She didn't teach me about Korean food; she taught me about Korean food *ingredients*. I was buying everything that I needed to make Korean food from scratch. However, I didn't have recipes per se, so it was just my version. At that point, I don't think you could call what I was preparing authentic "Korean food," but I was getting closer. As we continued to meet in H Mart, she taught me more and more, and she had me buy sauces and different ingredients.

It was like she was handing me a puzzle and making me figure it out on my own. Korean food is based on *bibim,* which translates to the word "mixed." It is about balance and harmony. Everything is carefully crafted to the elements of nature, represented by flavor and nutrition. For this purpose, there are main courses, then side dishes and soup that allow you to mix and create balance for each meal. How could this elderly lady teach an African girl all this with her poor English and my bad Korean? Well, love has a way of canceling language. She passed secrets from her culture. She gifted them to me, and I happily received them.

Like, did you know the secret to a good *kimchi-jjigae* is butter? In all my taste experiences, I had never thought about mixing butter with spicy food. The Halmoni grabbed me a premade kimchi jar. She spoke a bit to the manager in Korean before selecting one to give me. I now know she was probably asking him which of them had been sitting the longest. Then she walked me to the dairy section, got me some butter, and motioned with her thin fingers, showing me to mix it in. Oh, the charades of Korean cuisine we played!

Kimchi-jjigae is a classic Korean stew made from kimchi that has been aged. Aged kimchi tastes sour, but it's a good thing. To make the jjigae, you need pork belly sans skin, mirin (a rice wine), and aged kimchi. (Kimchi is a fermented napa cabbage side dish marinated in a spicy paste and left for four days to ferment like mintoumba.) For the sauce, you will need gochujang, garlic (always put too much garlic; *use one clove of garlic,* said no Korean ever), some soy sauce, and gochugaru (ground Korean chili powder).

Let the pork belly dance in marination heaven with the mirin for about 20 minutes. Then you cut your kimchi and add butter into a pan. You cook the kimchi, remove it, and put it into a Korean *dolsot* or stone pot, the same one you will eat from. Then, lightly cook your pork belly in a pan, but not entirely. Just begin the cooking process, and leave it on low.

In a pot, begin to make the sauce. In the dolsot, the butter will have made a thin coating. Place the pork in a semi-circle and add sliced squares of extra-firm tofu. Turn on the fire and begin slowly adding the sauce. Then add green onions and mushrooms. Let this all simmer until the meat is cooked.

Who knew at the time if this is how you made it? But this is what I had gathered from Halmoni. I showed her a photo, and she hit me really hard on the arm. I think that meant good? I went to have some kimchi-jjigae a few times in restaurants to compare, and it was close enough. I never measured; I just made it to my liking.

That was the first Korean dish I ever tried on my own. I felt so good after eating. I tasted it on my mouth, tongue, throat, belly, belly button, bottom, vagina, thighs, knees, leg hairs, ankles, toes, and soul! I was not hungry for a long time, and I slept so well—no wine needed. I even lost weight! I asked Halmoni if she could tell that I had dropped a few pounds. She looked at me and said, "No, too fattuh." She then pulled at my shirt and dragged me and the cart around the H Mart. She would never let me have any samples. *She cut me off!* That was my favorite part, but snacking at the market was out. I even came a few times during the week to add groceries but didn't sample at those times either. I was proud of myself, and I did not snack outside either. Therapy ended, and I was more at peace, or perhaps now that Halmoni was here, it was a good transition.

The Korean grandmother was showing me side dishes—*University of Halmoni*—and I could barely remember everything. I grew fond of her voice speaking in Korean. The language was soothing to me. Even when she spoke harshly or was frustrated with me for asking too many questions in English, I loved it. *How could I talk in Korean, Halmoni?* I don't even speak Basaa, my mother's language, which I yearn to do. But somehow, the intonation of Korean and Basaa sounded so similar I cannot figure out why. She continued to try to teach me in all the corners of H Mart.

They even sold Korean tableware there, so she was trying to explain to me what went where. The table setting is everything because there is always the main dish, surrounded by many side dishes—amazing side dishes called banchan.

You eat fish or meat and then have various flavors, fermented vegetables, and other sides to balance it all out. I had already been eating Korean food for years, but now that I knew where to shop for vegetables and ingredients, I was so psyched to go home and cook! I probably should have bought a cookbook, but I am terrible with measurements and precise instructions, and it just would have ended up sitting on my shelf. But learning from the Halmoni felt so right, and I needed her kind of love more than I realized.

I had no idea what I was doing. I was just trying to duplicate the side dishes I had tasted, fumbling through the best I could. The Halmoni and I had stayed at H Mart so long sometimes. She kept telling me to come there after "churchy." She added the letter "Y" to so many words; it was endearing. "No eat sandwich-y," "Go to church-y," or she added "-uh" to everything, "You must sleep-uh, drink-uh" and so on.

One day, I was watching *The Oprah Winfrey Show*, and she had Dr. Oz as a guest. He introduced the "Raw Vegan Diet" when there was a new push to bring vegan mainstream. There was the Al Gore *An Inconvenient Truth* movie, and Whole Foods opened in Manhattan. It wasn't mainstream yet, but it was for sure much easier to consider being vegan than ten years before. Vegan food started popping up in the grocery stores, and being vegan was beginning to enter into the mainstream American consciousness. But nowhere even came close to rivaling the variety of produce I discovered at H Mart. I mean, they had nine different kinds of mushrooms I never knew existed.

But this Dr. Oz episode on *Oprah* was wild because he had a large basket of vegetables, and he was saying that if a person ate all of it, they would lose weight. When I looked at all the produce that I had just brought home, I thought, *Oh crap! I have all of this. That's exactly what I just bought!*

That episode changed my life. Months later, I would meet Dr. Oz at an event, and years after that, I would go on the Dr. Oz show and thank him. While I had this Korean halmoni teaching me how to eat Korean style, I started on a raw vegan tangent. There was also Ani Phyo; she is raw and Korean, and I live for her. What I would do, though, is eat all my produce raw and eat it with raw fermented pickled premade vegan Korean banchan sides sold at H Mart. Always listening to and learning from the Halmoni, this combination made my vegan meals so tasty.

I also started eating like Koreans. For instance, I would eat everything wrapped in raw greens. If you go to a Korean barbecue, you stuff rice and grilled meats in lettuce leaves and eat it that way. Food tasted much better because I was eating the way the "Raw Vegan Diet" was designed, but the Korean sides, sauces, spices, and philosophy added delicious life and flavor.

Once I discovered this magic combination, my weight was dropping, and I started to step it up even more. I even started only wearing one sports bra when I exercised. I asked Halmoni, "Do I look thinner?" And she said, "So-so, ha!" We both started laughing. Then she slapped my arm again and said, "Wasting time!!"

Laughing then serious again, H Mart became an encyclopedia hunt for me. When you look at premade Korean foods, they are usually packaged in a small Styrofoam tray wrapped with cling film, with a white label listing ingredients and the dish's name. I started reading them to recreate the food. The labels were pure with simple ingredients like sugar, pepper, salt, etc. Those labels became my recipes.

I made sauces and ate them with everything. I started experimenting because the Halmoni made me buy soy sauce, sesame oil, and sugar. Soy sauce and sesame oil, with some sweetness, is like a heavenly combo of life—the perfect balance of flavor.

Eventually, I took white sugar out of my diet and replaced it with dark maple syrup. To Halmoni's credit, she did advise, "Sugar eat little-uh, no too much-y." I started to do minor substitutions, but not much because Korean food is so healthy. Honestly, being Korean and vegan is not much of a difference. Koreans eat so many vegetables with their food; it's practically vegan. But make no mistake, Koreans are *not* vegans at all. It's just that there is more than enough food to eat that doesn't have meat. The exception is fish sauce and banchan that contain it, but there are so many other side dishes that you don't even have to eat fish sauce if you don't want to.

I was doing more than just eating right, though. I tried to do all the things the experts were saying, but finding it went with what Halmoni said. I was drinking more water throughout the day. The Halmoni noted this too, and I learned that it is essential to weight loss. I also started reading Deepak Chopra, who would talk about Ayurveda, an Indian approach to healthful living, which doesn't endorse raw food. Ayurveda experts recommend eating cooked foods.

I was eating Korean soups like *doenjang-jjigae*, which is vegan if you make it with tofu. It has zucchini, tofu, onion, scallion, always too much garlic, and vinegar with a soup base of Korean soybean paste. I got the combination from a premade soup label made with pork, and I just omitted the meat. After I tasted this, I began making lots of soups using Korean miso as a base. Often, just this simple broth with garlic was all I ate, in addition to raw veggies with banchan on the side.

I lost 30 pounds the first month. After a year, I lost 110 pounds. I knew I lost weight when Halmoni said, "No, get too skinny. Eat more." I cried that day. She told me, "Stop crying." What a funny old bird she was! I loved us in our vacuum of the grocery store relationship. I bought her groceries each week, in addition to my own. All the Korean food was helping me stick to the diet longer than most people who tried to diet with raw food. She saved me. It became something I could eat for life. It wasn't a diet to me anymore—this was *MY FOOD!*

5

My time with the therapist had also gone very well. The food, the fitness, and the mental health were the work I needed to get myself fit for the love and family I so very much desired. In the end, she was analyzing my relationship with men; this was the final chapter of our work together. She showed me how I could process what I now realized about my life from our work together and how to utilize it to help make better choices with men. Or furthermore, how could I have a growing relationship with myself, and how would that help me make better choices in the future? The more weight I lost, the more I wanted to dive into my past and heal myself.

I spoke to my parents' friend, my brother's godmother, and she told me a very romantic tale of how my father was so romantic in the pursuit of my mother. Bingo! I wanted this too. Although it began to become less about getting a husband and kids and more about how I was starting to reshape how I felt about myself and forgiving myself for not letting go of the shields and masks I created when I was little.

Men, for me, was a very tricky subject. While I deeply craved a relationship, I acted the chaotic opposite of this. The men in my life have certainly been an interesting chapter. I'm grateful for all of them, but I played a ton of games. I'm almost scared to talk about this because there are people who I went out with and some whom I still know. They're going to be mortified when they read this, or maybe like John, at the Green Kitchen, they already know. But the story can't move forward without understanding this part of my life.

When I was dating, I had a trick. If the date was going well and I knew I would see him again, I'd find out his pet peeves. What were his dealbreakers? I'd use that information to end the relationship when I didn't want to go any further. On the way into the relationship, I was already looking for a way out.

It made the whole experience so much easier for me. If the guy hated smoking, I would store that information in the back of my mind. Then when he would get too close, or I thought it was time the relationship had run its course, I'd start smoking. If it were his dealbreaker, he'd break up with me, and our relationship would end. They wouldn't be as heartbroken, and I'd be out. It worked for everybody.

The therapist said that I was afraid of being broken up with. It was hard for me to understand at first because I was letting them break up with me. But my therapist pointed out that it was me actually breaking up. I was just letting them do it, and that was manipulative behavior. It kind of made sense, and I did try to understand this part about myself.

When I thought about it, I realized that I was just scared of being vulnerable and hurt. I would just annihilate the relationship, *kaboom!* Goodbye, gentleman caller. But the way that I did it was so crazy and not at all good. I could get an Oscar nomination for some of the things I did to make these guys believe they were the ones breaking up with me. I would act like it was hurting me, like I was fighting to keep the relationship, and it was tearing me apart that they were letting me go. When all along, it was exactly what I wanted.

I'd cry, "Don't break up with me! Please don't do this!"

This is why I'm so ashamed. If they find out, now they'll look back on that time and have a totally different perspective. It's embarrassing, but it was my twenty-something behavior, and that's my only excuse.

I had a girlfriend who was a Jamaican supermodel. She took me to an event in Harlem, where her friends were in a reggae band. At the time, I was still doing cause-related celebrity blogs for an MTV site called THINK MTV, where I would hang out with celebrities and talk to them about their causes and what they believed in. The model was the subject of my story, but I met this guy in the band. He was so skinny! He was vegan, and he was thrilled that I was going vegan. Plus, he was excited that I was affiliated with MTV. I wasn't some special famous VJ or anything, but musicians loved anyone having anything to do with MTV. It didn't matter if you told them you worked in the mailroom.

I started going out with him. He was so great. I credit him because I was just beginning to become a vegan, and he showed me up close and personal what it was like to live it daily. Through him, I saw how he lived. He was super healthy. It was challenging at times when we couldn't even go out to dinner because he wouldn't eat any of the food on the menu. Also, he couldn't eat it if it wasn't out of a clay pot. He was a Rasta, and I mean a real Rasta.

He didn't eat meat and kept his thoughts pure. He smoked weed. He was so gentle, and he showed me the lifestyle. He even invited me to live with him for a week to be entrenched in it and see it firsthand. That sounded good to me, and I was into it. It wasn't some sleazy pickup line. It was smooth like a true Rastafarian gentleman. So, I moved in, and I learned a lot from him. There was no sex; he actually was trying to help me. He didn't eat out very much. I was impressed by how he controlled all his food at home. Eating out of only certain pots also carried over into how he ate at home. That stood out the most, even though there was so much more to it than that.

But it was all good stuff when you're trying to lose weight or get healthy. Controlling your food at home is the best way to go. Even now, to this day, I eat more at home than I do out, so I am truly thankful to him for that. I stayed with him. We hung out, and I shadowed him.

He worked in a juice bar, and he had his music gigs. This relationship could have turned into something more, but my little fury turned on, which meant it was time for me to find a way out. It's always when I get too close.

I went straight for his dealbreaker. I pretended to eat meat again. It was the easiest way to get him to break up with me, and he was so cool about it. He looked at me and said, "What happened? What happened? What's going on with you?"

I knew what I was doing when I said, "Oh my gosh. I don't know if I can live like this. I give up."

He shook his head. "It's okay if you slip. Are you going to eat meat? Are you going to start eating meat again?"

I said everything that went against his principles. "Yeah. I just can't give this my all. I can't do it anymore."

He very kindly broke up with me and even sang me a reggae song as a parting gift. It was very touching. But that was the end of my story with the Jamaican guy.

I told the therapist about this one because it was with this guy that I started to be most aware of my behavior. Because he was so kind, and I thought I was doing such great work with her, how could I still be doing this? She said to me that healing wasn't a straight line. That with therapy, first I would be unaware. Then I would become aware and notice after I had repeated my behavior. Then I would be mindful yet do it anyway. At some point, I would become aware before I was about to do it and stop the pattern. Oh, wonderful, but at least I was on my way.

I told her about the egomaniacs early in my life before this pattern began—people who had taken advantage of me and who even hurt me physically. I never cried harder or as much as when I finally revealed the experiences that I decided made me a bad girl and destroyed me deeply. I won't repeat details; I reserve my right to hold some things close, except to say that *It can happen to anyone. Me too.*

Then I had a long string of Italians I dated since my best friend Greta was Italian. It wasn't that I was so into Italians, more I was always with them. When Greta moved to L.A., I stopped dating Italians. *Ha!*

Ironically though, the first Italian I ever went out with had nothing to do with Greta. I went to this basement restaurant called Pravda in Manhattan on Lafayette. It was this Russian-themed vodka bar. It was very modern, and they had latkes and smoked salmon. There was caviar—so much amazing caviar—and ridiculous Manhattan-sized amounts of champagne. It was just this sexy little lounge that everybody was really into. My girlfriend Candy and I remember seeing him from across the room.

He was sitting with people, but he was the only one who caught my eye. He was super handsome, as in movie-star good looks. I can't explain it any better than that, just a really good-looking guy. We were exchanging glances. I was getting this vibe from him, but he never came over.

Then, they simply got up and left, and I had nothing to say about it because I don't chase guys. Not now, not ever. I just don't chase men. But watching him leave, I thought if I were ever to pursue a guy… he would be the one.

Candy looked at me, and she just blurted it out, "You should have talked to him! Girl, you're so stupid."

I looked at her with a smile. "Nah. I'm not chasing dudes and starting a relationship off by chasing a dude ever." With all my messy ways, I got one thing right.

Candy shook her head. I could tell my answer didn't satisfy her, but it wasn't even a minute later that the waitress came over to me. She had a silver tray with a little card on it, and it was from him. It was his number, and it read, *I'm sorry I didn't come talk to you because I am with clients. Call me.*

I melted. It made me so happy! I loved the whole style of it, with the silver tray and everything. Candy, full Puerto Rican style, was like, "YOOOOOO… he's on some 007 shit!" It was just done so beautifully. I was still a freshman at NYU at the time, and this relationship was the most over-the-top romance I could have ever imagined. You have not been in a crazy romantic relationship until you've dated this guy.

He was an architect, not just houses, but major estate homes. He renovated houses you only read about in magazines. He had famous and wealthy clients who wanted him to custom design their estates and have him build them their dream home. He was so creative, and he was also this textbook romantic.

One time, he checked us into the Palace Towers on Madison Avenue. It was this super chic fancy hotel, and he had the butler bring all these trays of food up to the room. I was getting out of the shower, and there was this table with all these trays with silver tops. It was just like a scene right out of a movie.

But it wasn't a meal. It was just all these things that I like to eat, like olives and tangerines, kimchi, strawberries, gummy bears, plantains, and other random things. I can't even remember all the foods he had ordered, but they were not on the hotel menu. It proved to me that he listened to every little thing. It was a high-level romance.

Here I was still in college, and he was wrapping up on someone's house. He told me he wanted to take a break and travel the world after he finished this job. He had done very well in the stock market, and he sort of wanted to retire. He asked me if I wanted to travel with him.

I looked at him with a huge smile. "Oh my gosh, that would be so amazing." That was my first instinct, but I wanted to finish school. To this day, I'm surprised at how I handled this situation because of my personality. I'm really a travel-around-the-world type of girl.

But I chose to stay and finish school. Had I decided to go, money is something I would never have needed. However, I have met many affluent people in my life, and a lot of money does not a happy union make. Money or no money, a happy relationship requires something else. I had seen the look on many a wealthy woman's faces when their marriage was not that great. They weren't happy at all. Then the husband would leave the wife and take on a girlfriend, leaving the wife with nothing to do. Many had not finished college or had any job experience, and I had seen this happen many times. I had my mother in my heart. She would want me to finish school, and that's what I had to do.

I told the Italian all of this, and we talked about it. I asked, "Can we wait until I finish college? Then we can travel. Or we can travel between classes when I'm not at the university."

I thought we were so in love that breaking up wasn't even an option. But the next day, he took me to this restaurant called the Ocean Club on the Upper West Side, and while we were eating, he said, "I can't wait. I need to travel now. But what you're saying is so smart. You should finish school, and how dare I interrupt your search for your independence and yourself. I love you, and I want you to finish school. You're such a great girl, and you're right. But this is where I'm at; I'm going to travel now."

I was trying to wrap my head around this. "Wait! What? Hold on. So, if you're going to go and I'm going to stay, does that mean we're breaking up?" I was so crushed.

He looked at me and nodded. "Yes. That means this is over."

I backtracked and took back some of the things I had said, but he kept me to them because he knew I was right about staying in school. I was just so brokenhearted, and it hit me all of a sudden. I wasn't ready for it. It took me about six months to get over it.

I mean, this was the closest to a *real* relationship I ever had. I had introduced him to my sister Babs and my brother Bam Bam at a dinner in SoHo, something I just didn't do. I never introduced boyfriends to family. I thought there wasn't any point if I wasn't going to marry them. What a waste of time for people to connect, and then it's over—silly and painful. I was very selective. In fact, I only accidentally introduced one of my boyfriends to my mum because he went with me to an event at the UN. She met him when my mother summoned me to her office because you cannot leave a guest alone at the UN. You have to be with them at all times.

Anyway, that's how I was. I was very selective, but this Italian guy had gotten the best of me. I had introduced him to my sister and was planning on my mum next, on purpose. Now here he was, breaking up with me. I was so depressed. It felt like I lost a huge part of me. It was crushing. Perhaps that's what changed me? Because of this relationship and how it ended, and the egomaniacs who hurt me, I told the therapist I would never let anyone do that to me again. "BINGO!" she said, and that's where that all started. Wow, *all that* had shaped me into who I had become, the girl looking for the dealbreaker so that I could break up when I got too close. Because after him, there was no breaking up with me.

There were more stories: a Dane, a Nigerian, it went on and on… but the lesson was learned, and I was eager to move on with this newfound awareness. The sessions with the therapist ended, and I never felt freer. As she predicted, I did get better. When the urge came over me as I continued to date, I was aware, and eventually, I stopped the pattern. It didn't make every guy perfect, but I did stop the chaos, and sometimes I honestly now even broke up with them.

One time, a guy broke up with me, and it was wonderful. I wrote a whole email about it. It was a sign of my healing, and I was like, "Yay, thank you so much for breaking up with me!" He thought I was mad.

As time went on, each relationship became better and better. I would talk to God about it and say, "Wow, that was pretty close. Yes!" As I changed, I experienced the true power of a great therapist. It didn't take years; it was a few good months of work.

Because of this work, the quality of my time alone started to improve. When I was alone, I started taking care of myself. The loneliness began to lift, and in its place came grace. I found I needed to take more time alone. Being a person who connected to people publicly and also just a bubbly open energy-giving soul, I needed to use that alone time to be still and recharge—to live my life without the noise—and so I did. I began to meditate twice a day, exercise, and continue therapy. Because of that, the quality of my time with people also improved. I found I attracted more giving, wise souls, not people who just drained me of my life battery.

6

All the while, Halmoni kept nurturing me. She had me drinking so much tea, and that's from someone who spent many years in England where a pot of tea is always on. She repeated it over and over every time I saw her. Don't forget the tea! You have to drink the tea. She told me to drink hot water in the morning and throughout the day. But then, there was all this tea, and most of it worked on settling me down like a fire was being cooled, helping me sleep and wind down.

The word for tea in Korean is *cha*. I often drank *Omija-cha*, made with dried magnolia berries, but there were also teas with ginseng and some with Ginkgo biloba, great teas to drink while trying to get healthy or lose weight. When tea calms you, your mind can feel the other beneficial effects taking place in your body when you quiet down. It was like a program the Korean halmoni was putting together for me, and I had no idea what she was doing, but I found out there was a method to her madness.

The Korean halmoni didn't speak much English, but she taught me so much. I went happily to the H Mart on Sundays after church. She would be ready to show me more about what I should be eating to keep me healthy and get my weight down.

After a while, we had our system. Sometimes, Halmoni would ask someone to translate, but for the most part, it was just the Halmoni and me walking around the H Mart from aisle to aisle while she pointed at foods, and I put them in my cart.

I was filling carts up with shoots, squashes, red beans, radish strips, eggplants, *danhobak* (or kabocha, a green Asian winter squash), Korean radishes, Korean pears, lima beans, ponytail radishes, red chili peppers, Schisandra berries, soybeans, sweet potatoes, turnips, and walnuts as well as so many other kinds of nuts. I stopped fussing about not knowing her language and tried to drink in her instruction. All I knew was that she wanted me to eat them or prepare them somehow, and they would get me on track to losing weight. I learned the most important thing in Korean: food is love.

There were also so many greens. I had never seen so many vegetables in all my life. She had me buy chives, chrysanthemum greens, dried mung beans, dried split green peas, garlic scapes, green chili peppers, green plums, Kirby cucumbers, large green onions, napa cabbage, perilla leaves, radish sprouts, ramps, shishito peppers, and water dropwort. I ate them all.

I learned that ginger and cinnamon tied a lot of foods together and had healing properties. Ginger has medicinal qualities that reduce pain in muscles from exercise, helps with healing degeneration of the joints, lowers the risk of heart disease, and treats chronic indigestion. Cinnamon has similar medicinal qualities, effective antioxidants, incredible anti-inflammatory characteristics, powerful anti-diabetic qualities, and some studies show that it might protect against cancer.

Then *garlic!* So much garlic. If a Korean recipe calls for one or two garlic cloves in a recipe, Koreans will use a thousand. It goes on almost everything. Of course, garlic can keep you from becoming sick and help you heal if you get sick. But also, garlic reduces blood pressure and cholesterol levels that are responsible for heart disease. It's also great for a weight loss program, by the way. Garlic every day will keep you healthy, and it makes everything taste better. It's a no-brainer to include it in your diet. Variety and balance are the keys to health.

That merely scratches the surface of the foods she taught me. Dried persimmon, called *gotgam* in Korean, is loaded with nutrients and antioxidants. The Korean halmoni showed me these foods were packed with a powerful solution to aid my weight loss most effectively. Each was a piece of the puzzle. You can see how each food has its power, and some even doubled up to work in my body to make me healthier. I had more energy. My mind and body felt great!

All these foods were working together. It was like a puzzle at first for me to put together. I had all these ingredients but little idea what to do with them. I kept reading the labels on the premade food in H Mart. I ate things like a Korean food detective and tried to figure the rest of it out. But these foods work. They work together, and they are very effective.

The kimchi, though! I was in love with the kimchi. Don't think you have gone to a restaurant and eaten kimchi, and that's it. There are hundreds of ways to make kimchi. You make traditional kimchi with napa cabbage, and it's called *baechu kimchi*. If you've ever had kimchi in a restaurant, that probably was the one. But it goes way beyond that. For instance, you can make kimchi with cubed Korean radishes called *kkakdugi*. (Korean radish is called *mu*. Similar to daikon, it is shorter and rounder and has a green top.) Then, there's *oi-sobagi* which is kimchi made with cucumber. You can enjoy white kimchi called *baek-kimchi* or ponytail radish called *chonggak-kimchi*. *Nabak-kimchi* is radish squares, carrots, green onions, and napa cabbage in a pinkish-red soup. There's *gat kimchi* made from the mustard leaf.

You can make kimchi from anything. There is even watermelon kimchi made from the white rind of a watermelon. I could go on and on about kimchi and all the different ways to prepare it. I have eaten so many at this point in my life. It's a love affair. Anyone who knows me knows the deep love I have for kimchi. My gratitude to Korean culture for kimchi, as the door to health, will show in all I do.

I was eating kimchi all the time; I could eat kimchi in my sleep. I was eating it for breakfast, for lunch, for dinner, in the shower, in the bath…. She told me to eat kimchi for every meal, and that's what I did. I ate kimchi all day long. It's the only spot where my vegan years can be questioned because kimchi has fish in the paste and sauce. I didn't realize this early on until they started to sell vegan kimchi at H Mart. But it was too late. The positive effects surpassed the fish since I didn't know how to make it myself, and at that time, I wanted the *alive* feeling I got while eating kimchi.

So, I was a vegan except for kimchi. My house was like a forest of vegetables and fruit. I had lots of dried mushrooms and dried persimmon. If you've never eaten dried persimmon, do yourself a favor and give it a try. It's just like a pillowy soft donut with texture.

Korean food is so versatile. There are so many ways to play with seaweed sheets, a bit of rice, and whatever you fancy. The rolled-up seaweed with the cooked rice, strips of vegetables, and egg are what they call *gimbap*. Add to the diet the most delightful soups like *sundubu-jjigae*, a marriage between *dubu* (tofu) and kimchi, and you'd think there is no way I am on a slimdown diet eating this well.

At that time, what I ate most was the miyeok-guk birthday soup I told you about because it's so simple, just adding dried seaweed to water to make soups. The beauty is once you get familiar with Korean ingredients, you really can create several different soups just by swapping ingredients. Because of this, when one person makes you miyeok-guk, it'll have meat, and someone else will use mussels. I actually would just boil the seaweed in a veggie broth and eat this frequently. All the elements of nature combined nourish you in one bowl to heal your body. I learned that seaweed soup is beneficial for my thyroid because of the iodine, which though I never visited a doctor at the time, must have been out of balance. Eating Korean food is like listening to your body tell you where you are naturally. Maintaining balance and listening to nature is the beauty of traditional Korean cuisine for me. It is a food that listens to the rhythm of the Earth so well. If you listen to Korean food, you too can become in tune with nature. Just the setup of the Korean table is a sonnet, an honor to our environment. From deep in the sea to underground and overland, you will find all of these represented in the banchan.

Banchan is served in small white dishes on the table, ready to create your flavor balance. It is entirely up to you, as the master of your food. In Korean cuisine, you become a chef when you sit at the table because of all the banchan. You may have seven different people at the same table having seven different meals. One may go sweet, and the other spicy. It's a celebration for me. I feel the world should be like a Korean dinner table where each man or woman creates their flavor medley but eats the same meal together. I could never tire of eating Korean food because I don't think I've had the same meal twice. If you respect the traditional philosophy of Korean food, it is healthy.

Korean food ingredients are the foundation of health. Fermented and rich in probiotics, kimchi is vital for our gut health. Korean food is the governor of digestion and emotion. Learning more about how you eat Korean food will help you understand that weight loss isn't about losing weight per se but more about balancing your life. Not too sweet or too sour, not too bitter, and not always spicy, but rather all of these elements combined.

Most importantly, your life needs to be in balance first for you to heal. Weight loss is just one sign that you are healing if you are overweight, but it can also be a sign of illness. The point is to figure out the source issue first to find balance.

You must go to the source and take your time, just like how kimchi takes four days to be ready to eat. There is a lot you can learn eating Korean food if you listen to the lessons. Just as I was in the school of the Korean halmoni, learning about her life-giving food. I was on the verge of changing mine.

I even found this seminar by a Korean Buddhist who didn't eat meat and made mouthwatering dishes. It was a program at one of the Korean Cultural Centers. She made dishes with oyster mushrooms and lotus root. She even taught us how to make pancakes out of things like zucchini. It was amazing. Plus, she taught us how to make porridge. Koreans have a lot of porridge, which is so good; it's called *jook*.

One of my favorite things she made was a cold cucumber soup. Before that, I had only had gazpacho as a cold soup. But the Koreans have the most effortless cold soups that include noodles. One such dish is called *mul naengmyeon*, a chilled broth noodle dish. I never ate it for many years because it was made with beef broth.

I was slowly learning how to put everything together, and I was growing in my immersion, even eating at some Korean restaurants, which were gracious to make me mushrooms the size of a person's head, instead of the meat they served at the Korean BBQ. When I tried to explain my journey with Korean food, they would just nod and agree, "Okay. Okay. Okay." Then, they would bring me vegetables on vegetables. As usual, we became friendly strangers, and I believe my respect for them opened streams of kindness.

After a good meal at a restaurant, sometimes I would go home and read labels of premade food for hours to figure out how it was made. I would swap out things I couldn't eat as a vegan, then head back to the Korean restaurant and see how they made it, always and forever asking way too many questions. That's when I started getting creative.

On my journey, I was coming into my flow and freestyling recipes which I found out were not original but a result of my immersion in the ingredients—magical learning of Korean food by osmosis. Everything is already invented in this universe. God's design is universal, and that is how we connect. We think we are creating something new, but we only realize something extant. When we meet others that have recognized these same things, it's magic.

I found this truth years later when I came upon the story of a woman named Marja Vongerichten, a mixed-race Black and Korean adoptee who went searching for her identity with food as the vehicle. Her journey truly inspired me as I watched with wonder as she dove into Korean dishes, unlocking many lessons I believed the Halmoni was trying to teach me. I treasure her *Kimchi Chronicles* deeply. Watching every episode in great detail influenced how I cook. Also, seeing a black woman from that culture was new to me. She was so beautiful and brave. I remember wanting to know more about her.

7

One day after church, I went to the market, and she wasn't there. I looked around the store and outside. She was nowhere to be found! That's when I wondered whether or not these were official Sunday meetings. I felt let down and insecure because I had opened my heart. Had she? Did she know I'd come in today and just not show? Did she think of these moments the same way I did?

I asked about her. I went to the lady who sold me the bread that fateful day. She had no idea who I was talking about! I hadn't bought buttercream bread since, but she did see us every week. I said, "The lady! The Korean halmoni who had called me fat and handed the bread back to you. You don't remember her?"

She shook her head. "No. Sorry, no."

What? How could that be? I walked around the store and asked anyone who might have seen us together. No one knew who I was talking about. They did, however, acknowledge they knew who I was, which is what bugged me so much. It was like she never existed. I couldn't believe it. No one knew this lady who had come in this store, time and time again, and had taught me so much about food and helped me get my health back? I had lost so much weight during this time. The food was magical and all-natural!

But no one knows who this lady is? Come on! No one remembers her? We were the oddest couple of all time. I kept coming back to the H Mart at different times, hoping to bump into her. I had no idea what had happened. Perhaps she moved away? Or I started thinking the worst... maybe she had passed away? *Halmoni, where are you?* She had become my grandmother. Her name was Soo Kim. That's just what I gathered with my bad internet Korean compiled sentences to ask her name.

She was *Halmoni* to me, dammit! I had no idea how to find her. We did not exchange numbers, and she always stayed behind after. Also, I always bought her few grocery items each week. I offered to take her to her car, but she always said no. I went to the ladies at the small beauty counter where I bought Korean skin products. I had been working on improving my skin, too, and Halmoni was always with me. The K-beauty place is right after the cash registers. Surely she would remember. I bought so many products to jog her memory, and so she would be patient and not dismiss my inquiries about Halmoni... *nothing.*

Now that I'm thinking of her, I wonder what the surveillance video of us would show? If they had video footage in the store and I could watch it, I wonder if there would be two people walking around the grocery store or just me talking to myself? Were the people not talking to me about it because I was the crazy black lady who walks around talking to herself? *Had I imagined all that? Was she some kind of angel who came to help me and get me on track?* It's one of those things that sticks with me, and I never forget because of the enormous impression she made on my life. Now she's just a memory. It's sad. Thank God I said "thank you" to her a million times! I have what she taught me, and I have used it ever since.

Those lessons weren't wasted on me! To think that she had gotten me back to health and then up and disappeared when I didn't need her anymore. We met a little less frequently, but we would still meet. She was real. Anything else is a ridiculous thought, I told myself, and still do anytime I entertain the idea too long.

One night after looking for her and being completely deflated, I was in my flat and turned on the TV. Flipping channels, there was a show on Univision or some other Spanish language channel. One of those shows where the person is telling their story and actors were acting out the story. They had English captions. This one particular story was about a mother visiting a friend who lived on the third floor of an apartment building. When she checked on her daughter outside, she saw her on the stairs a few flights down. She was lying on the landing and was barely breathing. The mother ran through the apartments, knocking on doors to find help. Finally, one man came to the daughter's rescue; he was a doctor.

The ambulance finally arrived and took the daughter to the hospital. They took her to the ER, and by that evening, her situation was stable. She was fine. The doctor at the hospital told the mother that the actions that she took were right on time. If she hadn't done what she had done, her daughter might not have made it. But the mother told the doctor that she hadn't done anything, that there was a doctor at the apartments who had saved the girl's life. The doctor seemed confused because he was told the mother saved the girl's life.

I am not sure how much time passed, but the mother returned to that building to look for the doctor. She went to the apartment where she remembered knocking, but someone else opened the door and had no idea who the doctor might have been. When the mother asked around, no one had any idea. They all denied that a doctor lived in the apartment building.

The mother was so confused, but she was sure a doctor had rescued her daughter. She was there! She saw it with her own two eyes. The story concludes that she realized God sent an angel. I started to think about the Halmoni. Is that who she was? *Was she an angel?*

The following story was so outlandish that just as I began to question my sanity and the existence of the Halmoni, I felt so foolish even thinking it. The show continued with a man who saw Jesus in his breakfast and the Virgin Mary in his window. Thousands of people would come to pray to the Virgin Mary in his window. I turned off the TV, but the first story stayed with me.

Could the Halmoni have been an angel? Could it be that those kinds of things sometimes happen throughout our lives? We have angels who come and go. They get us through difficult times, and sometimes we don't even know. Maybe we aren't aware or open enough? One day, they are there, and the next, they're gone. All along, we were walking with an angel. I never talked to anyone about this except my mother. I wanted the surveillance tape so bad. Some days I still want to call H Mart and say, "You don't keep video now, do ya?" I wanted them to just rewind to one week when I met with her to see and prove she was there. *It wasn't just me walking around, was it?* A logical answer would be that maybe she had passed away, but that didn't add up either, as she was healthy and vibrant. She didn't act her age.

If God were to show us a video of our lives, *would we see these things happening around us? Are there things that we don't see that are happening to us? Are there things that we don't see with our human eyes that are part of this existence and this experience?* That is perhaps the answer we're looking for when we ask, what is this life all about? The unknown, unseen surrender of it all, when we release it to God, *do angels come?*

I must note throughout my journey with this mysterious Halmoni, as I was losing weight, I was walking more as part of my exercise. I even ended up giving up my car. I gave up the beautiful white ML320 Mercedes I loved so much. I worked hard until I got it, and it became part of my identity. It's horrible that it was such a part of who I was. Everyone knew that car, and I would be zipping around town in it, waving at people, serving the community, and always giving people a ride.

But I gave it up, and I was walking all the time. Then, I started running everywhere. One day as I was running, this idea came to me that I would set a charity challenge to lose weight.

The challenge was that I would attempt to lose 100 pounds and then literally run from New York to Chicago to thank Oprah Winfrey because I had adopted the "Raw Vegan Diet" from watching her show. It was more than that; she had also guided me for so long, living my best life. She had been showing so much love for African girls, which was so healing for me to see such a prominent figure place such high importance on the story of African girls. I also found out that Madame Winfrey had some Cameroonian heritage of a tribe in Cameroon called Bamileke, and so much began to click.

It was a series of clicks happening at once: the urge to run to Chicago to thank Madame Winfrey, and the Halmoni disappearing all of a sudden. *Or was she actually just me, helping myself? Or was she an angel sent by God? Maybe my grandmother had been coming to help me?* When I told my mother that no one was confirming that they saw us, she simply said that perhaps my grandmother Suzanne, whose presence I had been feeling so strongly at this time, was working through this woman to help me. I don't have any answers even to this day. I have chosen to remember her as an actual person and that my grandmother came to help me. The rest, though I want to believe, feels too far out to be true. Perhaps as I age and draw closer to my time leaving Earth, or through experience, I will find out the truth of that situation.

At the time of Halmoni's disappearance, I was very close to starting my charity run from New York to Chicago. I was planning to raise awareness for AIDS and education initiatives that removed children from at-risk environments. With plenty to do to prepare for the run, I had to move on from looking for her.

8

The run had become something bigger than me, and it no longer was about me anymore. I had made it about something else, something more significant. It was about service. It was about inspiring others to lose weight while also raising awareness about AIDS, and there were goals. I wanted to run the entire way to meet Madame Winfrey, and I wanted to thank her. I wanted to do it by my 30th birthday. Also, I was going to ask her for a hug.

People thought I was crazy. I knew it sounded like a crazy idea, but I was determined to do it. I just also knew that I was going to have to take some drastic measures. It was going to take some real training and commitment.

I had let the car go earlier that year. I had started walking, and then I joined a gym. However, the whole effort mainly felt like it was about me getting skinnier. While working with the therapist and eating cleaner, I had wanted to shift my intention. I quit the gym, and instead, I partnered with spiritually connected fitness gurus who were generous enough to donate their time in support of my mission. I called it the "Africa 101 Project," and my mission started to take on a much deeper meaning in my heart. It wasn't just about pulling myself back together and living my best life. I was effectively raising awareness for AIDS again. The activist in me was still there. Before, I thought being an activist was slowly killing me, and I didn't feel I could do it anymore. But as my mind, body, and spirit changed, I found it wasn't killing me. Instead, service was giving me new life.

The head coach of my team, whom we affectionately called "Team Africa," was Daniel Giel. Along with the late Sal Anthony, they founded the Movement Salon in New York in 1998. Daniel is a musician and a freelance performing artist, but he is also a movement guide. Daniel was who I wanted to lead this team because his training and exercises are so unique. His clients lose weight and get in shape, sometimes without even knowing or realizing it. The time goes by while weight is just melting off, and you look in the mirror one day and see a different person staring back at you.

Getting on the treadmill wasn't just for a run. Daniel had transformed using the treadmill into something else; he made me dance on the treadmill instead. The steps weren't just putting one foot in front of the other and going a set distance. It involved actions with my arms and different dance steps while keeping with the pace of the treadmill. We ran, danced, and jumped barefoot to music, and it was transformative.

Treadmills can be challenging, and they can get a bit tedious, but I will never see a treadmill the same again. It taught me that we could take regular life and, with a new intention, transform our movement to attract what we want in life. Thinking this way about how our body moves, as a carrier of spirit, is a much better way of exercising.

I also had the great fortune of being introduced to a man named Toby Tanser, who graciously came on as my running advisor. Greta had an actor friend in Toby's running group, and he told Toby about me. He is the founder of Shoe4Africa, an organization that uses sports to raise awareness for African issues, and has even gone as far as building a hospital for children. He is also the author of *Train Hard, Win Easy: The Kenyan Way* (1997) and *More Fire* (2008).

Toby didn't just make me go out to run for miles and make sure I made the distance. He got my body ready for the run. His training included running backward for long periods, doing high knees, and running sprints. It was awful. He is a very motivational man, and if you spend a few hours with him running, there is no way you're going to walk away from him and not be motivated. The best thing was that he changed my mind about what my body could do. That's the romantic version. The real truth: he had me throwing up after our first session in a running group he held in Manhattan. Then he would call me and tell me to get on a bus with only one-way fare, go twenty miles, and run home. His method, the Kenyan way to prepare for a run, is to run it every day. Then on race day, it's normal.

That was the training. After a while, I didn't even have to see Toby. I just took buses across New Jersey and ran back. The first time I did it, I left in the morning and came back at 9 p.m. It was so hard. My mind was saying, *This is bullocks. This white man is going to kill me!*

I called him and told him I was going to die from it.

"Well done, you," he said in his Icelandic, British accent. "Probably. I have to go." Then he hung up on me.

The following morning, he called me to ask if I was still alive. He was laughing and told me to do it again. "But don't come home so late this time; this is the secret to not dying." Another thing he told me was that I would never regret running. It may be hard, and some days it would be easy, but I would never regret running, which is still true to this day.

Ghylian Bell of the Urban Yoga Foundation was my yoga guru. Ghylian isn't simply a yoga instructor who comes to class and puts students through the movements for an hour. She is passionate about yoga and everything that it can do for an individual and the entire community. She instructs teachers and creates a curriculum that utilizes yoga to promote creative self-expression, character development, unity, and personal growth. To her, yoga isn't just an exercise.

From the Urban Yoga Foundation, I learned that yoga is so much more than a series of movements designed to improve strength and flexibility. Its effects extend into promoting many aspects of a healthy body and promoting a healthier mind and spirit. Plus, she did it with me one-on-one, and she listened to my body. She told me I could speed up or slow down a sun salutation, just as in life. Slow down when you need; go slower even than that. Fast is okay too, but not for long.

How could I lose? I had no chance of losing! With my team, the Halmoni, and myself, I was destined to lose the weight I had put on. However, I would gain so much more from the time I spent with these phenomenal people I had surrounded myself with. They were focused not only on my body but using it as a tool for a cause. They believed in me. They pushed me. They pulled me, and they carried me at times.

During a month of Pilates sessions with Daniel, I wept in the movement. I was so ashamed. It wasn't like the therapist's office, but moving parts of my body were releasing emotion. It was like therapy without words; it was therapy with motion. With this deep connection to mind and spirit in my workouts, I had no way of losing. It became complementary to therapy.

In addition to surrounding myself with these great trainers and inspiring gurus, I partnered with Product Red, Diamond Empowerment Fund, African Action on AIDS, and MTV Staying Alive Foundation. With this mission much more significant than myself and building every day, there was no option to fail. I was working out like an Olympian. I was working out almost five hours a day, sometimes even six.

I was still going to the Korean sauna in Palisades Park but chatting more as the years passed with the Korean ladies. They were giving me all this advice about different treatments. At first, they were like, "Who is this chatty black girl?" But then, they learned to like me. I was going about four or five times a week, but I was going on off-hours. There were only Koreans in there, and they were giving me so much advice about doing scrubs and massages. They had me doing herbal treatments. They got it! They saw it working, and they were on my side. They were trying to help me out as much as they could. It was as if the universe was orchestrating this massive amount of support in my favor.

One lady who saw how much I was coming saw that the treatments were working. She gave me huge discounts on everything because I was buying in bulk. I wasn't just trying out the merchandise; I was already sold on the merchandise. I knew it worked. If I was not training, I was in jjimjilbang or eating raw food, sleeping, or meeting with Halmoni at H Mart. This was the grand orchestration of my rebirth.

By the time I was ready for the run, I had lost 110 pounds in a year, and I felt like a warrior. I was doing the Toby bus runs much quicker, and I loved them. I would see an early bird *actually* catching a worm. I even once saw a flower open up and bloom. It was magic, and I was so light and bouncy. I was expecting Toby to train me how to run or how to put one foot in front of the other, but that's not what he did at all. He had me see nature, and I began to realize it reflected inside me. It was very in line with the balance and spirit of my Korean and raw food. *MASSIVE CLICK!*

I ran well and with ease. I took my time and experienced the changes as I ran through winter and then watched spring come. I had to run through winter to *really* feel that burst in my running come spring. I had to run through the summer heat to appreciate the running in fall. I had to run and rest. By the time I was ready to run, I had run about ten to twenty miles daily. It was normal. I wasn't about running fast; it was just about getting there.

I had a running coach before Toby, who spent three days teaching me how to put my foot down. She would correct me like I was doing this wrong or doing that wrong. Toby was completely different. He had seen all kinds of runners, from fat to skinny, short to tall. Toby didn't teach people how to put their feet down. He just told them to run. He told me not to use my headphones because runners need their ears. He taught me a bit about balance, and I would listen to him when he talked. But he was all about just running. *Just go run!* That was his training.

The day was finally coming for me to run, and I was cutting it close if I was going to make it for my birthday. I had to rent a car and drive to Chicago with a friend to map my route. Then fly back to New York, just in time for me to launch my run. That's how close I was cutting it. It was at this time that the Korean halmoni went missing! I was in the middle of the mission of my life. I looked for her, but I had to go. I couldn't keep looking back. I was on a strict timeline, and there wasn't any time to budge!

On September 15, 2008, everyone gathered at the United Nations to launch the Africa 101 Project. In attendance were some really big names. I was surprised to see how many faces showed up to offer their support.

The media came, and Kevin Liles, the Vice President of Warner Music Group and author of *Make It Happen*, actually gave a speech for the launch. It was inspiring to hear him speak, listen to what he had to say about my project and me, and what I was trying to accomplish.

Bertil Lindblad, Director of UNAIDS New York Office, also gave a speech. He acknowledged not only the problems with AIDS in Africa and around the world but also my part of raising awareness and my contribution to the fight against AIDS. The activism that had been killing me and the stress I had felt only a short while ago was now gone, and I was being acknowledged for my ongoing work against a deadly disease—only this time, I was healthy!

New York City Mayor Bloomberg sent someone to speak along with a message for all the mayors I would meet on my run. That was a very kind gesture from the city I loved so much!

Then my sister Teresa showed up. I remember looking up, and I was so surprised to see her there! As we walked from the press conference to where I would start the run, she grabbed my hand and held it quite tight. She is a tough cracker, and it took me by surprise. I said, "What's this?"

She said, "I'm worried about you, man." She continued, "Be safe out there." I felt so loved at that moment. I will treasure it for all my days. She showed up!

I didn't just run for me, though. I wasn't just running for my own Africa 101 Project. While I ran, I endorsed Product Red, founded by Bono and Bobby Shriver in 2006 to raise funds for the Global Fund to Fight AIDS. I met Mr. Shriver at an amfAR gala in New York. He was extremely kind to me. It's a pleasant relief when people you look up to are good people in person too. The Diamond Empowerment Fund was building schools and educating students in countries where diamonds are a rich resource, and I endorsed them.

All this was made possible by MTV, who provided me with a platform to shout out to other organizations raising awareness, raising funds, and helping people in any way that they could. It also provided me with a way to reflect on what I was going through at the time. Each step of the way, I had MTV viewers reading and watching a unique video blog we created and looking at the pictures we published en route.

Along the way, I fell in love with small-town America. With over 1,000 miles to run from UN Headquarters in New York to Harpo Studios in Chicago, I ran through many small towns, and I fell in love with them all!

Despite running into the KKK in New Jersey and Ohio, I met many more great people overall. One night in Ohio, I had dinner with the head of an LGBTQIA high school group. This young lady and her family looked at my map and warned me about certain towns along the way. "Don't go there, black girl! That is not the area for you!" I made the wise decision to reroute and run around some areas I had initially planned on running through.

In New Jersey, I stopped at a flag shop because I wanted to buy a UN flag. Oddly enough, they had one. I had this bright idea because I was getting press along the way. Up ahead, there was a bridge I would be crossing into Pennsylvania. I thought, wouldn't it be great to run across with the UN flag?

While I was in the shop, my friend Candy, who has much lighter skin than me, was told by the shop owner, "You better get your friend out of this town, or she's going to be going out in a body bag."

Candy looked back at the shop owner like, "What? What's going on?"

The shop owner said, "She's going to confuse a lot of people running with that flag, and running! Why is she running? She's going to confuse a lot of people."

Candy came out to the car and said, "We have to get out of this town now."

There were three of us in the car. My other friend Anson, who was also black, was with us at that point, and we had no idea what we had gotten ourselves into. We left. On our way out, there was this trucking company that had "Lynch" in its name, and I'm not trying to say they lynch people, but we took it as a sign to get out of that town as soon as humanly possible. Racism in America is alive and well, and the racists aren't afraid to tell you. People think it's gotten better, but it has not. Racism in America still exists, but many more people embrace different cultures, and I am one of them.

Suddenly, everyone has a camera, so it seems there is more racism than ever, but black people know this simply is not the truth. It has always been like this. We feel it in the system. We feel it in the street. We feel it every day.

As I said, I met many more great people than I did those who were against me. That made the run even that much more important. While I was running every day, I would try to get ahold of Madame Winfrey's people when I would stop to rest. There were people also writing letters on my behalf to get ahold of her. Tony Eason, a yoga guru from San Francisco, held a fundraiser with his class and sent me new trainers when mine wore out.

I was getting closer and closer to Chicago. My birthday was coming up on Monday, but on the Friday before my birthday, it seemed like meeting Oprah Winfrey would not happen.

My mother had flown in from Cameroon by this time, and she looked at me with this serious look. "Are you kidding me? You just ran from New York to Chicago. You ran about more than double your intended miles and lost 110 pounds. I'm not going to let you summarize your achievement by needing one person to congratulate you, even if we do love that one person. Your experience is not summarized by meeting Oprah Winfrey. Keep your head up. Finish your run and be proud of that run."

I repeated those words: "I am proud of this run, even if I don't meet Oprah Winfrey." I looked back at her knowing she was right. But I had one more thing in me when I said, "Okay, all right, I'm going to do one last thing. Is it okay if I just make one last effort? Then I'll know that I tried everything to contact Oprah Winfrey. Then I'll leave it. I'll just run, and I'm going to feel good."

It was starting to get cold. It was November, I was feeling cold, and I was just at the end. So, I called *The Oprah Winfrey Show* mainline, and an operator answered. My attitude was different, though. I was letting go of this and giving it to God. I was in surrender, so I had this whole different attitude about it. I just simply said to the operator, "Hi! Can I get the PR department?"

Every time we had called before that, they never transferred me. But this time was different. The operator said, "Please hold."

She transferred me through, and a girl picked up. "Good morning!" I said. "I'm sending a fax. Can you kindly give me the number, please?"

She said, "Oh okay, please send it to…," and she gave me the fax number. I had to memorize it because I had no pen! I was totally in shock that I was finally getting an actual number. I had not prepared for that part. God, your magic is every single breath and always present when we surrender all to you, this I know.

I mean, a year of trying, and I could never get through. There was always some block or issue, and I never got through, but this time was different. I felt like at least God was giving me a little more than what I was used to when I couldn't get through at all. So, I sent the fax from the hotel where my mum was staying.

I had the best run ever in that crazy cold weather! I started to put all those lofty goals behind me to meet Oprah Winfrey and get a hug from her on my birthday because my mum was right. I had just accomplished an amazing thing, and that's what was significant. When things don't always go your way, it's what you achieved despite it all that's important. You can count those accomplishments. What a magic ride healing myself, and it felt good to let that all go.

All these people were coming up to me while I ran that day and saying, "Hey, I heard about you!"

I was surprised. "Really? You did?"

There was a mother whose daughter was overweight, and she asked, "Can my daughter run with you? I heard about you."

I looked at her with a strange expression. "You heard about me? How?" Was there some bootleg PR video getting out there? How had all these people heard about me?

I allowed the girl to run along with me, and all these people started joining in. There were people taking selfies with me along the way. It was odd because I had stopped doing PR for a while. I had no idea how my story had gotten to all these people. This run was crazy, but it was crazy in a good way. I loved it! The universe public relations department of GOD was on the job, as usual, carrying it further to people than I could have on my own.

When I finished the run and got back to the RV around 4:44 p.m., I jumped in the shower, and a call came through. My mum was hanging in the RV, and she answered. She yelled to me in the shower, "Telephone!"

I came out with a towel wrapped around me and answered.

The voice on the other end said, "Hi! I'm calling from *The Oprah Winfrey Show*."

I lost it! I couldn't believe that I had finally gotten through to her. She continued, "Would you like to come and be a guest in the audience on Monday?"

I was stunned. I asked, "Monday? Are you kidding me? On Monday?"

She answered, "Yes, on Monday. Is that a problem?"

"On my birthday, Monday? On the day that I said a year ago that I would run from New York to Chicago and get a hug from Oprah on my 30th birthday. That day? That Monday?" I thanked her and was in tears, but she thanked me for what I had done. Oh, God! You are the one and the truth. I speak your name.

I asked if I could bring my mum, and they told me I could. Tony Eason had come, and he stayed in the RV with my dog Tesoro. Tony truly is such a uniquely special man who put a golden context to all I did.

That morning, I woke up early. The only part of my run left was from that parking lot about 500 meters away to Harpo Studios right up the street, one block over. I ran and finished the run. I wanted to do that alone. I ended it on my own just as I had begun, in the dead silence of the morning. I was so proud of myself. I had so much energy in my body. I could feel the bottom of my feet vibrating as if I could take off and fly if that's what I wanted to do. Then, I ran the last part of the run again later at daylight, and Getty Images captured it.

When it was time for the show, I got there early to stand in line. It took a while, but I was finally admitted inside. As soon as I got in, though, I had to go to the bathroom. A lady was sweating profusely. I felt bad for her because she was so excited about being at the show, but she was embarrassed by all the perspiration staining her armpits. I was trying to help her dry up the sweat. All my crazy ideas worked! I can't even believe how happy I felt assisting her. When I turned around, a group of ladies applauded me, and my mum was laughing. She knows about my yearning to serve and how these kinds of things happen to me. The up-closeness with people I never met, for the sake of love.

But that's when I heard the announcement over the intercom: "Suzanne Africa Engo! Please come downstairs. Suzanne Africa Engo. Come downstairs at this time!"

I had to get down there. As I walked into the studio, it sounded like they had mixed me up with someone else because someone pointed at me and said, "Oh, that's not the runner. She's the runner."

They had a special chair for me right offstage, but they had put someone else in it because it was her birthday, too. When they tried to switch her out, I could see how happy she was to be in that chair. So, I said, "No. No. No."

I found another seat, and then the audience warmer came in and asked if anyone had any announcements to make. The audience blew up. There were people having birthdays and celebrating anniversaries, and everyone was making an announcement. I couldn't bring myself to do it, though. I felt like it would have been an ego thing if I would have stood up and announced, "I just ran from New York to Chicago!"

It probably would have blown all of the other stories out of the water, though it wasn't more important. I just didn't say anything. I didn't want to show off or make anyone's special day less. That's when the audience warmer looked at me and asked, "Hey you, why aren't you saying anything? Tell them why you're here!"

When I announced it, one lady shouted that she had seen me running earlier, and the audience started clapping. They asked, "Why did you do it?"

"It wasn't about fitting into my jeans. It was about fitting into my dreams." I don't know where that came from, but it just popped out of my head, and everyone went wild over it.

When the show began, I completely forgot the reason I was there. I was so happy with everything I was learning on the show. I was just enjoying being in the chair I had seen so many times before from the other side of the TV. The show went on from guest to guest, and as it wrapped, it was starting to sink in. "I did it!" I finally just let go because I had done it. I had accomplished everything I had set out to do, and I just let go. I did my work. Let go and let God, right?

That's when Madame Winfrey was asking if anyone in the audience had any questions, and then she started reading from the prompter. "There is a lady in the audience who ran here from New York. Suzanne Africa Engo?"

It blew my mind. Imagine that for a moment. It was a million to one shot, and I did everything I could physically do to make it happen, but it wasn't all up to me. I couldn't make Oprah Winfrey meet me or invite me to the audience. That was in God's hands, and all my dreams were coming true. My mind was racing. I couldn't hear anything, but she was saying my name, and that was too surreal.

I stood up and started talking. "I just wanted to run here and thank you. I watched your show, and I started the 'Raw Vegan Diet.' It helped me, and I'm just living my best life."

She looked at me and said, "I didn't say you had to run from New York to Chicago!" The audience laughed. She asked me a ton of questions like, "Where did you sleep?" and "What was it like?"

I answered her questions, and then I remember myself repeating, "It wasn't about me fitting into my jeans. It was about me fitting into my dreams." I went on to talk about raising awareness for AIDS and being an activist. I could see that one of the guests on the show, Dr. Michael Beckwith, was nodding, and he mouthed to me, "YOU GOT IT." Then I finished what I was saying, and I sat down.

Ms. Winfrey shook her head and said, "Don't sit down. Come up here. You've come a long way."

I looked at my mum, and she looked back at me like this was freaking us both out. She was so proud. I live for these moments I make my mother proud. You have no idea all she went through so I could dream, so the system didn't bruise me too hard. She is a celebrator of "us." I walked up to the stage, but I kept my head together. I knew some Hollywood people don't like touching or hugging. They don't like getting too close for whatever reason. So, I didn't expect that, but I wanted it. I played it out in my head. But when I got to the stage, she put her arms out. She gave me a huge hug! I just about lost it; it had happened. On my birthday, after my over 1,000-mile run, I had gone to *The Oprah Winfrey Show* and met her. Not only that, *I was now hugging her!*

It was too much. I was overwhelmed, and I just started crying. The photographers took a picture of us. I was a little too much in the moment how it had all come to pass. Oprah looked at me and said something to this effect, "You worked hard for this. You want to remember it right. So wipe your tears, and don't have an ugly crying face. You want this picture to be good." She has good advice, that all-mighty aunty. She had her arm around me, and I had a huge smile. After they took the picture, I bowed to her, and she put her hands together and bowed back. I bowed lower than her to show respect as the Koreans do. Then I went back to my seat, where my mum was still in shock. To be honest, I was too.

9

It's hard to explain, but I loathed the return to New York. I drove back with my mother, and I couldn't get into it. My body felt uneasy, and the vibe made my stomach hurt. My life had changed so much over the past year. I wasn't into the same things anymore.

I got invited to a fancy dinner at the headquarters of Hearst Magazines, and an event at a nightclub. Ellen Haddigan, the head of the Diamond Empowerment Fund, graciously invited me to the events. I truly treasure Ellen Haddigan in a way that cannot be explained in one book.

I asked a new friend, Cassie, to go with me since she was a pop singer and she'd draw attention to the cause. She had just helped me draw attention to a program at GMHC (Gay Men's Health Crisis) before I left, and she was gracious and came. Lots of chic people were there. Kim Kardashian and a young lady named Ms. Carla DiBello were very kind to me that evening. Ms. Kardashian wrote a blog post about my run and its mission. Tamsin Smith, the head of Product Red, was there and big stars attended this dinner. Even though I was very grateful, all I can remember was that there was something about the environment that I just wasn't into anymore.

I canceled my festival, the New York AIDS Film Festival, because I just couldn't begin that whole energy again. Believe me when I say we had some huge names lined up. But once I'd healed for real, it was hard to eat again what made me sick. I had great energy, and I was not giving that up for anyone. I didn't want to do the festival anymore. I was supposed to have this big arrival when I came back to New York, but I just didn't want to plan anything. I wanted silence.

I had accomplished this monster thing, and I was just done. I wanted a new chapter, but I didn't know what that chapter was going to be. I had been doing this isolation running for so long. I was too used to being in the wilderness running. I had spent all that time training, and I spent a lot of that time alone in quiet reflection and quiet solitude. Quality solitude had replaced loneliness, and it was my favorite place. New York was just too loud. The more I thought about it, the more it became overwhelmingly loud.

One of the foundations threw an event at a nightclub and invited me. They were so kind and gave me this five-star treatment. After I arrived, they announced that I had just done this run for their charity, and they told everyone in the audience about everything I had done. They gave me flowers in front of everyone and celebrated me. It was a special moment.

Then, I remember this red carpet night that was done up with a green carpet, and they were selling these green bracelets. As I was walking the carpet, there were flashes everywhere, and everything was so bright. I took my friend Ghylian, who had helped me train, and I remember saying, "This is really bright, and everything is so loud."

I mean, I had been living in an RV for two months and in isolation the whole time. I wasn't used to all this attention, the noise, or any of it. Friends said, "Darling, come over for dinner and let's celebrate all your running."

I didn't even want to do any of that. I was getting invited to dinner a lot more because of what I had done, but I remember thinking that I just didn't want to go to any of them. I didn't want to be anywhere unless there was a real reason.

I had changed. Paul Simon, the singer, had warned me, and he was very prophetic. Before I ran from New York to Chicago, I was blogging for MTV, and Wyclef Jean was putting on this major breakfast event thrown by Hugh Locke. There were supermodels and actors, activists, and VIPs of all kinds. I had gone to blog about the event, and I ended up leaving at the same time as Paul Simon.

We ended up talking, and I told him what I was planning on doing. Mr. Simon listened and said, "You're going to run? From New York to Chicago? You know you can take a bus or hop on a plane, right?" It was a funny moment. But then he said, "Well, whatever happens, you are going to be transformed when you come back. So, get ready. Make sure you are ready for that. You are going to be a completely transformed person."

That's exactly what happened in those days when I arrived back in New York. I realized what he had been saying was true. My weight loss and the meditation, the Korean spa, and the Korean halmoni who originally changed my diet—it was all true. I wasn't the same version of me anymore. The New York

City life and the flash of all the parties and the events simply had no significance. Not only that, I just wanted to get the hell out of there. The only thing left of my New York life before the run that I had any more interest in at all was my Korean spa and my Korean food. That was it.

I did finally attend a red carpet again. This time, I was there full of purpose. After I ran from New York to Chicago, I ran again—from Italy to France and then later across Cameroon and parts of South Africa. It was the year of the 2010 World Cup in South Africa. I decided to run. This time, I was not only raising awareness about AIDS but also informing people about solutions that I felt would help remove kids from at-risk environments. For instance, in South Africa, there was a school where many children had scholarships, but many of them lived pretty far from school. So, I ran from one of the girls' homes to the school to show people how long it would take her to get to school every day.

It was virtually impossible to do. Madame Oprah Winfrey understood this very well and sponsored a dormitory for girls at the school. I slept in the dormitory and not a hotel while in South Africa to be with the students. It was one of the most magical times of my life. I told the girls to clean the dorm and keep it clean to express gratitude to Madame Winfrey. They should never let it get dirty or slummed. We had a whole cleaning session together.

One of the sponsors of my run was a woman named Sally Morrison. I had met her in the bathroom of a charity event in New York, where she complimented me on the African headdress I was wearing. She spoke with a British accent, and she invited me to an event a week later. I didn't know who she was. When I arrived, I realized that this woman I met was one of the most prominent forces in the movement and quite powerful. Who would have known her powers? She was so humble and down to earth. Even as I saw the lovely actress Julianne Moore present her with an award, she was elegant and modest with her young son in tow; truly a class act. I thought, *Wow, that's true power, to have it and still be kind to someone in the loo!*

Well, Madame Morrison took me out for lunch, and she asked me what I needed. She ended up supporting me on my run, including getting me a single seat at a very famous gala called Cinema Against AIDS, which I would attend when I got to Cannes after running there. It was most helpful toward meeting key people committed to fighting AIDS, and it was nice to have a good sleep and a pleasant evening to celebrate all the miles before running in Africa.

Before I left for Europe, I was in a dress shop in Manhattan to buy a gown for that event. While I was trying on dresses, I got a text from my mum saying to call home. Well, since you don't know my mum, I'll let you know she does not text. I was instantly worried as my papa had been unwell. I dropped the phone; it took me several tries to pick it back up. I called Mum, and she told me my father was dead. I started to scream, and I grabbed the first dress I saw off the rack. The shopkeeper said, "Wait, that is the dress you said you hated."

I didn't care. I said, "Please, just charge me." I ran into the car, and Armando, a wonderful man who used to drive me at that time, asked me what happened. I looked at him and told him Papa was gone. I went home, and I went for a run in the night. I ran so long I didn't come home until 1 a.m. I called my mum as it was morning in Cameroon. She told me that I should do my run. Because of political timing, my father would not be buried right away. She also said she would wait for me to bury him because she felt he would want me to run. I didn't want to, but I agreed. I also never thought about that dress again until I arrived in Monaco.

The Monaco part of my run was supported by a man named Elio Locatelli, Director of Development at World Athletics. He had found me a small apartment for my stay in Monaco as I ran that portion of the run. He also noticed I was limping and told me that I would see the athletic doctor of the Prince of Monaco, and it was arranged for me not to pay. The doctor fixed my ankle up and told me to rest for almost a week. This is when I opened up the dress bag and found the blue dress. It was awful. I zipped it back up and didn't think of it again.

When I arrived in Cannes, I was really proud of my accomplishment and decided to wear my dress with pride. I arrived on the red carpet and decided to smile my way through it. I met Kevin Frost, the CEO of amfAR, on the red carpet. He was a lovely man, so kind and gentle with me. I needed it. He was telling press cameras that I was an important activist. It was nice of him to do so.

I was there with purpose, and I thought little of the ugly dress. I was more focused on my trainers. Converse, a partner of mine at the time, gave me these trainers where the proceeds from their sales went to fighting AIDS. So instead of having the press focus on my dress, I lifted it to show the sneakers. All of a sudden, the less-than-interested cameras started shouting for my shoes. They were so loud, but the cacophony was fun. It felt good to be winning in raising awareness. Many people complimented me for wearing comfortable shoes.

I walked into the Hotel du Cap, where the event is held annually. There are massive stairs, beautiful as if from a movie. I walked to them, and I saw an elegant man standing, looking out at the view. He turned, and it was Tom Ford, an American designer who I admire for his talent and integrity. The most important thing to know about him is that he is the king of the fashion world. It was at this moment that I began to think about the awful dress I was wearing. When I saw his face, I thought about jumping behind someone or jumping and rolling down the stairs *007*-style before the hotel blew up behind me. It was too late. He saw me, and our eyes met. I walked a few steps closer, and I greeted him. "Hello, Monsieur Ford." I might even have curtsied; I was a nervous wreck inside.

He said, "Hello," and gave a warm smile.

I continued, "My name is Africa Engo, and I have just run from Milan to Cannes, raising awareness about AIDS."

He said, "Well done, that's important. Thank you."

I said, "Well, I know I am terribly dressed to meet such an important person in fashion."

He replied, "Well, it isn't the dress that makes the girl, *is it?*" It was an actual question, and he waited for the answer.

I spoke. "Yes, sir."

He replied, "You look beautiful. Have a good evening." It melted my heart. Wow! With that, I turned to the stairs and walked down, smiling large and feeling like Naomi Campbell. Until the real Naomi Campbell walked by and said hello. So yes, not Naomi Campbell, but I think being there with a purpose and stating it made the moment go well.

Also, Tom Ford will forever be a king in my eyes—not of fashion, of kindness. You never know who you are meeting or what is happening to them, as it was with my father at that time. A cruel word would have crushed me that day. I was paper-thin inside. Instead, because he was kind, I walked confidently around that night full of purpose and feeling beautiful in that dress. Many good things happened that night, and I will always be grateful to Madame Morrison and Monsieur Ford for the steam to shine.

Again, when I returned, I avoided my friends, and the running created a need for me to be on my own. This continued for years and did not end until recently. I just disappeared, like the Korean halmoni. Was I even real? I had to be defined by myself and not outside sources to protect my energy and listen to God's plans for me. Having no friends is so interesting, but I began to find the pieces of me in the silence. The work was deeper than shedding weight.

I started working on a documentary about my run because I wanted to have a record of it all. It was tough piecing together television-quality footage, which made it hard to get on the air. Christina Norman, who had been president of MTV, went to work at the Oprah Winfrey Network and let me submit it. They loved the story, but it wasn't broadcast quality. I was okay with that; it didn't hit me hard. Christina introduced me to the new president of MTV, who decided to put it on MTV.com, giving it its own unique page. I became the first feature-length documentary on MTV's site, and I stayed there for a decade with a special dedication to my energy. Times were changing, and being online where I could easily share it became the best place to be.

While finishing up the documentary, I started writing many songs about my experience—something from childhood reemerging, songs and poems. It started taking shape as a musical. A mentor of mine suggested Louisiana as a place for me to be creative. It was more fitting of the artist in me reemerging. I rented an apartment and moved to Louisiana and a completely different lifestyle.

I moved to the countryside to write. I had finished the documentary, and I was free. So, I started working on a musical. I was so happy in Louisiana. It was slow. I was in nature just as I wanted. It was the exact opposite of what I was used to before. All these things became my values.

I got phone calls from friends, and they tried to make plans with me. "Come to New York for the weekend. We'll have so much fun. We'll do all the things. Are you flying in for the gala?" I just wasn't into it anymore. I used living in Louisiana as an excuse to get out of seeing people. I had no more interest in doing those things.

I liked being with solid, grounded people like my trainers. I was becoming more like them. The champagne and red carpet life weren't my things. Not that they would never be again, but there had to be a real purpose or inspired feeling for why I got myself up and went somewhere. From grocery shop to gala, *why am I going?* Because lord, let me tell you in New York or L.A., they will invite you to the opening of a shoebox, and you have to learn to say no.

I was into the small towns of America. I was even thinking about moving to different small towns like those I saw when I was running through Pennsylvania. I spent a good year and change in Louisiana, finished my musical, moved to New Orleans, and was just hitting my stride there. Then the beautiful queen who was renting from me had a life shift and had to leave all of a sudden. So I returned to New Jersey, not wanting to but truly happy to have found that I could find a place that fit who I was now.

Ellen Haddigan of the Diamond Empowerment Fund invited me to her wedding in Chicago. Years before getting invited to that wedding, as I was losing weight, I learned about the Transcendental Meditation technique, or TM for short. An older lady in my apartment building in New Jersey had been teaching me some things about TM, but she said she wasn't technically qualified to teach it. She encouraged me to learn from a licensed teacher. She told me about an Indian guru who taught her and a small town in America where many people gathered to learn TM.

She had cassette tapes of him speaking, and I would listen to them on her old Sony Walkman. As I was losing weight, I sat for twenty minutes twice a day in silence and listened to all these tapes—sometimes having transcending experiences, other times not. While I ran, I thought about what I had learned and whether it would be the key to having that bliss every time I meditated.

I learned that while I would be in Chicago for Ellen's wedding, I could get an introductory course from a licensed teacher in TM. So, I made an appointment with a woman named Carol Morehead. It was a definite upside to the whole trip, not to mention seeing my dear Ellen again. That made it easier for me to make plans to go to Chicago.

The story gets a little strange at the wedding where I sat down with this lady, Melanie. Melanie came from the same small town that the lady who originally introduced me to TM had told me about: Fairfield, Iowa. It wasn't only that. Melanie had learned TM from Maharishi Mahesh Yogi, who was not only the guru for the Beatles but the same one I had been listening to on the cassette tapes. In 1974, Maharishi moved the Maharishi International University (named Maharishi University of Management from 1995-2019) to Fairfield, Iowa.

I was so surprised by this strange coincidence. I looked at Melanie and said, "You've got to be kidding me. Are you for real? Is this for real?"

Melanie ended up inviting me to Fairfield, Iowa, to meditate with her. I didn't even have to think about it. It was just too perfect of a situation for me. It felt divine, and I was looking for meaningful steps.

I am not one to stay with people. So, I thought I would find a hotel or a place to rent and then visit her. I logged onto Craigslist to look for temporary homes. Instead, I was seeing lovely places to live in Fairfield for about $500 a month. When I thought about it, all I had to do was give up my gym membership and storage in New York and New Jersey. Those two things were enough to afford $500 rent in Fairfield, on top of the monthly maintenance on my place in Jersey. I didn't have to find a renter or buyer to do this. I was determined to move.

My mum came to visit from Cameroon, and I told her about my plans. It really all made sense to me. I was ready to move, and even if it sucked, I'd come back to New Jersey and use my Fairfield apartment for storage. It didn't matter. My mind was set.

I packed my car and drove with my dog Tesoro, sight unseen, to Fairfield. Melanie went to check out my new apartment and said it was a dump. It was too late, though. If anyone knows how to take something from dump to darling, it's me. I just made the arrangements and went. What I found was a spacious dusty apartment. I had to clean, but it was massive. I hired a maid and her crew. She was drunk the entire time she cleaned, but she got it done by the end of the day. My friends said I was crazy for moving to the middle of nowhere in the corn, but it was my life.

There was a different dynamic to Fairfield. It was a small town, but people were coming from all over the world to live there, drawn by the energy and pull of the work of Maharishi. It was so chill, and everyone was into TM. It was just this remarkable place for me to be at the moment. It also had a strange mix of people. There were "townies" and the "roos," short for gurus, referring to the meditators. Sometimes they got along, sometimes not. I was happy with my decision, but I had no idea what was about to happen.

10

I was driving to Fairfield, Iowa, with all my stuff, to an apartment I'd never seen. Before I left, I thought it would be a bad idea to date in a small town. I had watched enough movies to know that could go bad, really fast. Girl breaks up with guy, sees guy on the corner at the only store in town and every day while running. So, that was out. I thought maybe I would put myself online and look in nearby bigger cities. I did still want to be married and have children, so that's what I did.

I picked Match.com, the biggest site. I figured it would have the most options. I created my profile, and that was just before packing my car and leaving for Fairfield. I put about seventy-five pictures on there and didn't write much. Then I got in my car, and I was off with my Yorkie, Tesoro. Along the way, my phone started blowing up with notifications every minute. I was getting all sorts of hits because apparently, I was popular in the Midwest. Who knew? I just kept getting hits as I was driving, and it was getting annoying because it would interrupt my music in the car. Plus, it was obnoxiously distracting. That's not good while driving; no phone and driving for me.

When I pulled over for gas, tons of guys had sent me smiling emojis or waves. I was flattered but wanted them off. I wasn't that focused on dating at that moment. I hadn't even gotten there yet, and I was on a mission to do the drive within two days. Before I left, this one random girl I met said her brother had a friend who lived in Iowa, and we connected. The friend's brother hit me up, and we decided that we would meet up when I got to Fairfield. He was away on business, but we started texting, and we were getting quite flirty.

I just wanted to get to Fairfield and figure out how to turn off these notifications on my phone. Since I did not have the internet on yet in my new loft, I had to find some free WiFi in Fairfield and sit down at my computer to figure out how to turn off notifications. As I was trying to figure it out, there was this one guy who caught my attention. There was something about him. Mostly I could tell he was Korean.

I was surprised that there was even a Korean in Iowa. I didn't even know if there were going to be black people in Iowa. A Korean in Iowa piqued my interest. Besides, he was cute. I messaged him back.

I told him that I was just getting into Fairfield and settling in. I wasn't going to be on Match.com that much, and he should use my personal email to get ahold of me, which he did. I was just settling in, and I had no idea how fast it was going to happen. I wasn't ready quite yet, and he kept messaging me. In fact, he asked if we could *meet*.

I thought that was a little too fast, so I wrote back, *Whoa! Hey, internet guy! Slow down. Shouldn't we talk a little bit first before we meet?*

When he replied, he gave me his phone number and asked me to call him on Thursday. *If that goes well, maybe we can meet on Friday?*

I thought about that for a moment and wrote, *That sounds like a plan. We'll do that.*

Days were passing by as I was busy finding dancers for my musical, and I found someone who came to audition. She was great. I also found a young man to work with me to film the workshopping of my musical's choreography. I got busy fast! That's the New Yorker in me, able to create a life and work. Thursday came and went. I completely forgot about calling him because I was so excited about turning part of my new apartment into a dance studio and working on the dance part of my musical.

When I read my messages on Friday, there was a message from him. *Hey, you forgot to call me yesterday. So, are we still meeting? Because I don't live close, and I'd have to leave now.*

I was doing yoga with a new friend in my loft, and I told him about this guy I had innocently forgotten to call. He looked at me and said, "It's a small town. There really isn't much to do here. You might as well go."

I wrote the Korean back. *Okay, I'll meet you.*

I made a plan. There was this one restaurant I noticed that was super empty. If he was not for me, I would take him there. If I liked him, I would take him to this other nice restaurant. It was above a seedy bar. After you walk past the bar, the restaurant was one of the nicer ones in town. You just have to walk through the bar to get to the restaurant. That's the one thing about it.

We met at a Verizon store, which is random. But that week, when we messaged, he suddenly said his phone broke, and I thought that was weird. We emailed about that, and I asked him about his broken phone.

I was just suspicious, as I always am. Why wouldn't he just buy a damn new phone? I was also wary because of the whole internet dating aspect. Some people who tried online dating told me that they never talked to the guy on the phone. That's weird. Why wouldn't someone call if they liked you?

But now I know why… he can fix a phone himself. He's this techie who knows how to do those things, and he hates to spend money when he can fix it. In fact, meeting at Verizon was perfect, and he messaged me from there since his phone wasn't working. It was pretty interesting what he was doing. He used their system to get a text to me.

When I walked into Verizon, all I saw was this super beautiful man in the middle of Fairfield, Iowa. It was a heart-skipping moment, even though I yelled at him for the first five minutes of our date. Because after he told me how he had hacked the store to get ahold of me, I wasn't happy about my personal information being on Verizon's system. But we got past that part because he was so good-looking.

He had beautiful kind eyes that closed like bird wings, and when he blinked, I missed his eyes and couldn't wait to see them again. His skin tone was sun-kissed with black hair. He was in great shape and looked better than his pictures. I never read his profile.

As we were leaving the store, he put his arm out like the old-fashioned way couples walked down the street in the movies. I wrapped my arm around his, and he made his arm strong. I felt like things were happening slowly, and I tried to take every second in, like a meditation. I wanted to be right there with him, present in the moment. *Hi, whoever you are. How did you get here so fast? I've been waiting for you, forever, I think.* I was looking at him as an investigator of spirit. Everything about him was different, and he was Korean American! That wasn't anything I had ever imagined, not because I wouldn't, but only because I hadn't ever dated a man from Korea or of Korean descent before.

I remember us talking at dinner. It was the most comfortable conversation. There were many pauses, and in my mind, silent applause when everything he said just fell softly on my ears. There were no awkward moments. I remember laughing and enjoying what he had to say. His hair was so full and bouncy. I silently thanked every fool of a woman who ever let this majesty slide by them. *Could this be my love? Is this the moment, without announcement or spectacle? Has love arrived unto me?*

"...in their hearts, humans plan their course, but the LORD establishes their steps..." Proverbs 16:9.

I remember I had been reading a lot of Rumi at that time and decided to do what I read: "Close your eyes. Fall in love and stay there." That and leave it to God.

I felt so at ease with him. I always wondered what on Earth married people talked about all day. Not today, at dinner; we spoke like we had known each other all our lives. We were so relaxed with each other. When he looked at me, his eyes looked like they were breathing a sigh of relief. I looked him in the eye, and I did too.

I don't usually let a date last longer than an hour and forty-three minutes. That's my limit. After that, it's too long. I know how to make guys fall in love with me. Then just like that, the old instinct kicked in. The need to play my old games awakened, even though I had been so good. But with all the work I had done, I recognized it and cooled it instantly. I wasn't going to do this, not with this guy. I had to respect the "inner knowing" I was experiencing—that magic moment we all dream of. All that I had been through had led me to love. God answered fast in my heart, nudging me forward.

"...those who hope in the LORD will renew their strength. They will soar on wings like eagles; they will run and not grow weary, they will walk and not be faint..." Isaiah 40:31.

I knew right then and there; this was it. I did it. I actually did it with a lot of prayer and steps. I found the love I craved. It happened.

I remember going home after the date and being so happy. The date ended magically. One of the things I had prayed for was that I wanted to get flowers from my beloved. While losing all that weight, I bought myself roses once or twice a week from a flower vendor in Manhattan on Houston and 6th Avenue after my sessions with Daniel. They had this eternal two dozen roses for 24 dollars sale. I bought myself so many flowers that one time a friend came to my flat, and there were so many flowers that he asked, "Have you been nominated for a Grammy and didn't tell me?"

At the end of the date, the Korean asked if he could walk me home. I told him no. My loft was only steps away, but I said no and that I would walk him to his car. He pointed to his car, which was parked nearby.

He said, "I have something for you anyway." He opened the back seat and had not one but *two* flower bouquets for me. I wanted to cry. No one ever gave me flowers at the end of a date before. So different, timed so perfectly and chic, and he smiled this big, warm smile at me as he gave them to me. *How does his face have room for all that smile?* It was an immense beauty; how grateful I was that even once, the source of a smile like that was me.

When he asked to see me the next day, I told him no again. Then, he asked if he could see me on Sunday. I had already made plans for that day, so I told him no again.

I could see him getting frustrated, and I thought, *Let him chase. Don't kill him, child.* So, I spoke, "Fine, I have some time on Sunday morning."

He jumped at it. "Okay, I'll take it." Then, he held my hand and asked if he could kiss me. Oh, the manners! Old-fashioned like I like it… and it was the best kiss. I tried to pull myself out of it, but I couldn't. *Toss the rules when the kiss is so good.* It was perfect; it was *love!*

Though in love, wisdom could not be thrown out the window. I ran a background check on him the first chance I got—a very thorough international-diplomat's-daughter-level check. When I received the results, I was thinking, *Phew. He didn't kill anybody in Spain.*

Our second date was at my flat. This is rural Iowa, where there aren't a million things to do. I wasn't too sure about it at first because just as I was thinking how perfect everything was, he told me he had a dog, and he was going to bring her on our second date.

"You what now? Why?" *Ugh!* And the dog looked big. I'm African. It took all my might and facing my fear to get my dog, Tesoro, a small Yorkshire Terrier, and not be scared of him. See, Africans don't have dogs as pets. We have them as guard dogs. When he showed me the dog's picture, she looked huge, and all my dog fears came back. I thought, *This is what's gonna do it, boy. The dog!*

But I agreed because I thought I didn't want to block the blessings God sent. Imagine, *God, I want love. Okay, here you go. Sorry, not good enough. Dog is too big. Ha!* Better sooner to see what this dog situation was early. I had planned on cooking at my loft, and I was unsure how our dogs would get along.

My loft was nowhere close to finished yet, and I set the table up to eat sitting on the floor. That was the way I had been eating, and I didn't think anything of it. I had sat this way many times at Korean jjimjilbang and loved it and had even designed a floor table for my apartment. It was a comfortable and relaxed setting, and I made all this Korean-style food.

If I had to describe what I had prepared, I would say I made a vegan version on *samgyeopsal.* Okay, even just writing a vegan version of samgyeopsal is ridiculous. There is no comparing. I will continue anyway.

Samgyeopsal is a grilled pork belly meal where people grill sliced pork belly and eat it with banchan in a lettuce leaf. Samgyeopsal means three-layer flesh. *Sam* is the number three in Korean; the name refers to the three layers of the pork belly when sliced. Well, I didn't eat any meat at the time, but I suppose I had three types of vegan meats? Mock vegan duck, tofu, and mushrooms which are often eaten with samgyeopsal.

Usually, the meats are grilled with garlic and then wrapped in a lettuce leaf. I had no grill, but I had collard greens instead of lettuce, some salted sesame oil—something I have come to cherish—and gochujang. There were also green chili peppers and *sigeumchi*. Sigeumchi is a steamed spinach banchan, easy to make all over the country since spinach is widely available. It is steamed with sesame oil and garlic. I was primarily raw vegan at that time, so there were many other raw fruits and vegetables in small dishes, all things that I ate regularly. When he saw it, he looked at me, surprised. "Wow! Did you do all this for me?"

That's when it dawned on me that he might be thinking that I made Korean-style food and ambiance to impress him. So I said, "No, this is how I eat." Then I told him about that part of my life with the Korean halmoni, and our conversation just intertwined like a *kkwabaegi,* or Korean twisted donut.

I asked him a whole bunch of questions, and he asked me just as many. Am I religious? What are my interests? We just kept going back and forth between each other, and then he got on the topic of his deal-breakers. He was telling me all the things that would turn him off about someone.

I remember listening to him for the first time being nervous like, *Oh boy, I hope I don't do any on his list!* Butterflies fluttered in my stomach. Luckily, it was a pretty short list: God in, cigarettes out, drugs out. *Phew!* I actually wanted this to work and not try to get out of it somehow. I was hyperaware of that and proud of myself.

And the dog? Lucy was the sweetest dog, so loving and cuddly—my first daughter. I asked for one true love, and God sent two. It seemed that the Korean was here to stay. We both felt the exact same way. No one was too fast or slow, just at the very same pace.

In fact, I canceled my plans I had for later that day. I was supposed to go on a date with that girl's brother's friend. We had been getting along great on the phone, so canceling really baffled him.

To clear up the confusion, I decided to tell him why I was canceling our date. "I know it sounds crazy because it's so soon, but I think I found *the* guy. I really like this guy I just met."

He was super classy about it and said, "Man, one week earlier, you would have been my girl. Lucky guy. And if he doesn't work out, call me."

I never did call back. Things moved fast with the Korean. He took charge and knew what he wanted. I loved it. I was calling him "the Korean" because I was referring to him that way to a new girlfriend I had made in Iowa the first day I moved there. I went to walk Tesoro in the evening, and I met a woman out trying to exercise. Tesoro and I were bouncing around. She said, "I guess that's how you stay so skinny?"

I asked how, and she said, you two keep moving a lot. I told her I had been there with the weight. Kathy and I became fast friends. She was who I confided in about the Korean. That's how we referred to him: "Oh, the Korean guy this" and "the Korean guy that." The way women do. "Oh, how is Connecticut guy," or "banker guy," or "Oh, are you seeing red tie guy again?" A way of referring to someone before it gets serious. Like Carrie referring to her Mr. Big in *Sex and the City*, minus the crushing heartbreak that followed. Then she was asking me how things were going with "the Korean." We said it so much that this stuck as a nickname.

I remember telling him that, and we laughed. He went in my phone as "The Korean" and stayed there. He is also a bit more private than I am, so referring to him as "the Korean" provides a bit of anonymity.

He invited me to his place to spend the weekend in the city—Iowa City, to be precise. Spending that much time together, we found out so many things we had in common. His parents were immigrants who came from South Korea. Despite the difference since he was born in America, we both had parents from somewhere else. There is a commonality in that experience, no matter where you begin.

Even though I told him some things about my history growing up and the Korean things I learned, he would still teach me Korean stuff, and I loved it. Sometimes he would laugh and say, "You're more Korean than me." To which I replied, "Impossible! African to the bone."

That was one of the things that drew me to him the most. I already experienced some things about his culture: the food and the spa side of it anyway, which translates to home life. We also had a shared interest in having and keeping it in our lives. For me, it was convenient that someone would be interested in eating Korean-inspired food every day. So while we were finding out so much about each other on this third date weekend and realizing how into him I was, we had this "financial summit."

We talked about everything we owned and how much money we had and made. We talked about our debt or lack of debt. It was a conversation I had never had with anyone else. We put it all out there, and here I was, just ten days living in Fairfield! I was already making plans with a guy I had just met. That's how crazy this whirlwind was, but everything was also so serene. It wasn't how I pictured true love coming; it wasn't some grand sweeping thing. It was very calm and easy, but how I felt on the inside was far more than I imagined I would feel. He was everything I was dreaming about, but better. I had arrived from that desperate place depressed in my apartment so long ago to here. It was almost like all my time with the Halmoni prepared me for this love.

I remember discussing details about my apartment in New Jersey and my apartment in Fairfield. I had found a tenant to move in for a one-year lease, and I was going back east that Monday to get the rest of my things. He was driving me back to the country and telling me how much he would miss me, and then he looked at me and said, "I don't want to wait. I want to start now."

I looked at him crazily. "What? What do you mean?"

His eyes softened a little as he looked at me. "I know now I found the person I want to be with for the rest of my life, and I want to start that now." Bumps ran up my arms into my heart and dropped softly there.

All I could think to say at the moment was, "How?"

That's when he said, "Let's move in together."

That blew my mind. I was like, "What? Are you serious?"

This conversation was taking place ten days after I had just moved to Fairfield. It was weird, but I felt the same way. I was right there where he was. I wasn't famous for relationships, and then here I was rushing in. I wasn't a let's-move-in-together-in-ten-days-girl, no matter how much I wanted love; I was not that before.

But he wanted me to move in with him and, while in love, I was too empowered for that. So, I said, "I'll do it, but you have to move to the country."

He looked at me with a straight face and nodded. "Fine."

This couldn't have been crazier but oddly well-timed. His lease was about to end, and he was about to renew but hadn't. He could get out by not signing, but he had to vacate before the end of the month as the new month started in one day, which was also when I was supposed to leave and drive to get my stuff. "If that's the case, I have to get all of my stuff out of here in twenty-four hours, or I'm going to be obligated."

I know more about him now and the way he is. He is always on time. He is super organized, and he doesn't let things go. It's very odd that he'd forget to resign the lease his landlord left for him. He's never late! Maybe the madness of meeting a crazy African girl delayed his usual process?

So, here we were on a time crunch. He had to be out in a day with no wiggle room for negotiation. His favorite part was my country-ass rent. "Five hundred bucks, can't beat that!" he said. We also rented the other apartment across the hall to have the whole side of the building for 800 dollars. Which, even two apartments later, was way less than he was paying in the city. *That might have added to the love right there, ha!*

My plans got flipped upside down. I was going to go east with a small truck and get the rest of my stuff. Kathy was set to go with me, but I had to tell her, "Hey, remember the Korean?"

She said, "Yeah?"

"Well, here's the deal. He's going to move in with me."

"What?"

"Yeah. So, the thing is… I have to get his stuff out of his apartment and into mine by the end of the day tomorrow and alone because he has to go to work for a big meeting he can't miss."

The look on her face was priceless. "Are you serious?"

I nodded again with a resolute look on my face that was beaming through my smile. "Can you switch the truck and ask the guy to give us a bigger truck? Then, we need to take the truck to the city and get his stuff."

"This is insane and romantic. But, yes."

So, she got a larger truck, and off we went—right back to his apartment. The funny thing about it was he hadn't been planning on moving, so not one thing was ready. He had been planning on signing a new lease for the following year. Our plans had changed all that, but he still had to go to work the next day.

Here I am, with this truck and going to his apartment to pack him up while he was at work. This was our fourth date! One in a nice restaurant above a seedy bar. Two in my apartment eating Korean food on the floor. Three at his place for the weekend. And our fourth date was me packing his stuff to bring to my home.

I got into organization mode, and I went through his apartment lightning fast until I got to the back room. Everything else was minimalist and easy. But that back room? That's where he had everything else he owned. But I barreled through and got him out of that apartment by the end of the day. Then, off driving east, I went to get the rest of my stuff. I mean, let me tell you something. Nothing else in this world has proven to me how organized I am, quite like packing a stranger's house I am madly in love with in less than a day. Oh, but in the middle of it, I got on my knees and thanked God. There was nothing I would rather have done than fold his shirts at that moment; it was bliss.

I got my new tenants moved in and returned to Iowa with the rest of my stuff. It was all so fast, but it was all just right. He called me and checked on everything and got us a hotel room to rest on the drive there and back. When I got back home, he surprised me. He had worked on the loft. He had painted the walls the colors I wanted. He had listened to me and was so considerate. It was so romantic. Everything I had said about the loft in conversation was in progress.

We lived in a renovated 1920s J. C. Penney Company building. It was a small building and sweet, but the apartment was quite large. Here I was walking up the side steps to the loft, and I remember thinking about the man I love on the other side of the door. After all these years alone, someone is living with me now. I opened the door, and two dogs immediately ran toward me, almost knocking me over while a strong man started walking my way. I felt so loved and complete. It was everything I ever wanted and so much more.

I never knew what it would look like, but I was guided to this wonderful place. *Nothing that is meant passes by; it's coming, it's coming.* I consider him to be the first man I ever loved and even truly my first real boyfriend. At that moment, I realized that all those times before, I never even knew what love was. A real relationship, committed and true, is quite something extraordinary.

Soon after we settled in, he wanted me to travel with him because he said that a couple isn't a real couple until they travel together. So, we planned to go to Thailand. When we talked to our families, though, his parents were in Korea, and my sister Babs, who I am very close with, and her family lived in Hong Kong. They all wanted to see us, especially Babs, who thought of me as her bachelorette sister for life. We thought we would go to Korea for two days, and then Hong Kong for two days, and Thailand would be somewhere in the middle. But both our families thought that was too short, so Thailand got dropped altogether, and the trip became just Korea and Hong Kong. I guess African and Asian families have that in common. They are pushy, and they usually get their way.

I was super excited. I always wanted to travel to Korea after all my experiences. Also, my parents had been there and brought back lovely photos and stories. My sister lived in Asia, so it wasn't my first time in Asia, just never to Korea.

Everyone was warning me about Korean mothers-in-law. They were saying, "Koreans hate black people, and she won't like you," but I knew the history. I knew what it was about. One person even told me to have a hotel ready in case I needed to leave. I did nothing of the sort. Why would they invite me to stay at their house if they were racist? That's the first thing that would not have happened. They had seen my photo. This wasn't a surprise visit where they discover the fiancée is black at the door. Second, there's no way they could have made such a lovely human with hate in their heart. I chose to believe otherwise, and I also decided not to tell any more people I was going so they didn't drain my energy.

We finally arrived at the airport in Seoul, and there she was, the Korean's mother. She was tiny and beautiful. His father was handsome, thin, tall, and strong. As we walked toward them, she and I stared at each other for a minute. For both of us, it was our only chance to stare without being impolite before we reached each other. The Korean hugged his parents. It was lovely as they hadn't seen him in a while. Then she and I just looked at each other, and then we both just broke out in laughter for some reason, and we hugged each other. From then on, we were tightly arm-in-arm; she held my arm like my mum and I do when we meet at the airport. Anything that reminds me of that Queen mother of mine was a good sign.

We went through the airport and then got on a bus to their flat. When we arrived, his mother and I took off our jackets, and we were wearing the exact same color clothes. We were like twins. It was so weird and so funny. For that, there was even more laughter. I love her laugh. Like the Korean, not enough room on her face to hold its massive beauty.

We are a lot alike. She is a talented painter. She even had one of her paintings featured on a stamp. She is a tiny ball of fun. We are both artistic, and we are both traditional. Sometimes art suffers for tradition and responsibility.

For the first meal at their home, we washed up and then came to the dinner table. It was my birthday, and my mother-in-law prepared a completely Korean and vegan meal for me. A whole spread—"No meat-uh, no fishy... beegun, all beegun"— and my eyes welled up with tears I never let fall.

"You made me a vegan meal? Thank you so very much. That is so lovely and kind of you."

That meal will go down in the history of my life as the most honored food I have ever eaten. There was zucchini, lots and lots of vegetables—some I had never seen before—and tons of mushrooms. She made a doenjang-jjigae made with Korean soybean paste, garlic, onion, zucchini, tofu, mushrooms, and pepper, but she sliced small potatoes into it. I never had it with potato. I was learning so much just eating everything; I ate so slow everyone was finished eating, and I was still there.

She said I was healthy to eat slow, every word so encouraging. She could open a restaurant! It was beautiful. Wow. For her to make a meal like that and remember that I was vegan said everything about who she was. It was the warmest welcome I have ever received. Then at the end—a cake. A cake I knew was made with eggs and dairy things I did not eat. The Korean knew as well. The three of them sang happy birthday to me, and I grabbed my plate and a large piece of cake after. I ate my first dairy in years, and there was no way I was going to say to her, "I'm vegan; I don't eat that." I wasn't going to die from eating cake, which I had eaten all my life up until a few years back.

This is a prime example of the Korean concept of NUNCHI: To gauge what the other person is feeling and act according to this unspoken knowledge—emotional intelligence. No matter how open and well-mannered, you have to know that to a Korean of a certain age, interracial marriage is not usual at all. You have to give credit that they chose to love and have an open heart. They are my elders, but at that moment, I thought to myself how proud of them I was. Not because I think anyone should get an award for not being racist, but because if you have any sense of history, you would know how much work it is to go against the wave. So, in nunchi, I ate the cake.

I said, "Thank you so much," and was actually glad to soften on the raw vegan routine. It was the first bite of finding the true middle balance of what and how I would eat in the years to come. So, I am forever grateful for that cake. After dinner, I told her that I wanted to call home as my mum and I always speak on my birthday as a tradition. They said they wanted to talk to her too. "Wow, okay!"

I messaged my brother to come to my mother's room. Here I was, in Seoul, on a Skype video call huddled around a screen with the Koreans looking at my other loves in Cameroon, my mum and Bam Bam. Everyone was smiling; everyone was laughing. Dr. Yoon, my father-in-law, had read about Cameroon, and you could see that. I couldn't take it; my heart was so whole. They talked, and I was just looking at my brother Bam Bam, and he was looking back at me. I could tell he was really happy for me.

Then we got off the phone, and we exchanged gifts. I had brought them African gifts to thank them for having me as a guest in their home, and they gave me birthday presents. The entire night was out of a movie I had never seen in my life—just something else. Then the Korean and I went to our room and them to theirs. I hugged him so hard I think I cut off the circulation to his head temporarily.

Then his mother came into our room and was sitting on the bed giving me all these things like pants with tiny flowers on them (by the way, the most comfortable pants I ever wore in my life). She gave me slippers and pillows. Her energy was so motherly and delicious, full of love and positive energy. It's funny; the Korean is a lot like my mother, and I am a lot like his. At the end of that dinner, Dr. Yoon turned to me and said,

"I see that my son is going to marry Mommy," because she and I are so alike.

He also said, "I give my blessing and welcome to the family." I couldn't hold that tear in. I had to let one drop. I wiped it quickly and said thank you in Korean, and bowed my head slightly lower than his.

I went to the bathroom after everyone slept that night. I got on my knees, looked up, and said, "Thank you, Daddy," and all the tears came down. That was all the speaking I could do; all the thank you washed down my face. I tiptoed out of the bathroom back to bed. As I did, I looked at where I was in this flat, a world away from New Jersey and even further from Cameroon. I just took it in, grateful for every morsel of good fortune that was upon me. Self-love leads to true love.

She would wake up so early and cook. It made me realize just how much energy she put into feeding her family for so many years. At five in the morning, she would be up prepping like a restaurant chef. She did that every day, and I was up and willing to help because I run very early in the morning. That is how we bonded, with her cooking and me helping and learning. I took photos to remember small things, and she would just teach me. We connected quite well. We didn't go out much in Seoul because I was in this culinary academy of hers. She's a master of cuisine. I told her just to teach me and not make it all vegan so I could see how it is done. She still made me vegan food the entire stay, but I got to see her make many recipes.

My favorite was mung bean pancake, which is magical. It's the Korean's favorite. His grandmother used to make it for him. You take some peeled yellow mung beans (his mother says you should have a few green ones, too). You soak them in water for a few hours, or you can put them in water when you go to sleep. In the morning, they'll be good and soaked through. Wash them and put them into the blender, and they will blend into a batter. You may add a little water so they are blended smooth. It looks sort of like when you make American pancakes—not too runny but not too thick. Then chop up green onions and kimchi pretty small but not minced. She never gave me exact amounts. I just looked on and eyeballed what she did. I never cook by measurement; I just use my senses to get it balanced. Add some chopped bean sprouts and mushrooms, and you can salt it if you like if you're a veg head or some pork belly or other meat if you are not. Mix it up, pour it into a pan, and flip when browned. That is how you make *bindaettoek* or *nokdu jijim* which is literally "mung bean pancake."

It went on like this the entire time I was there. She goes all day and her hands hurt, but duty carries her forward. I was soaking in so much, and the Korean's mother was filling in many of the holes I had from the Korean halmoni.

So many "Oh, that's what you do with those!" moments I remember having. It was thrilling. I watched ever so closely the art of the Korean woman. It's a lot of work those women do to hold their families together, and she does it with so much grace. Food was our whole relationship. I think mothers-in-law can love a daughter-in-law who worships them as I do her. But it wasn't put-on or fake; I genuinely think she is an amazing woman, and I happily listened to her as she told me to chop this or that and "Only Jesus" at the end of every sentence. "Yes, yes, more kimchi and God. Amen." No arguments from me there.

When she came to visit us about six months later, all I wanted to do was get her to relax. So, I got her a massage. I had Kathy come to the house. She is a first-class masseuse par excellence. Besides jjimjilbang, it's the best massage I have ever had in the whole world. I put a robe out for Mrs. Yoon and then was ready to head to the other apartment to give her privacy.

When I called out to her to see if she was ready, she flung open the French doors and started motioning like she was a boxer being announced into the ring. My robe was way too big on her. She was making fun of the fact that she was only 4'11" while I was 5'8" and showing herself in this massive robe. I think we laughed for about twenty minutes straight. Kathy was like, "Wow, you two are like twins."

There are so many stories about families that don't accept mixed-race couples. Even if you never focus on it that much, you hear about it. I feel so blessed for all the love from my mother-in-law and my father-in-law from the beginning.

My father-in-law was also quite a funny guy. The Korean says that he never heard his father talk so much as he does with me. I think that's just because I'm chatty and I ask lots of questions. I think it forces people to talk a little bit more.

I have tattoos down both my arms. So, when we were in Korea, that first trip, I thought I'd wear long sleeves the whole time out of respect for my in-laws. My mother-in-law was very appreciative that I was wearing long sleeves, and the Korean was also. My tattoos are quite understated but still, for older generations... I believe they deserve respect. I can show my tattoos elsewhere; I don't have to prove anything about who I am.

One day when we were sitting at the dinner table, my mother-in-law and I were still getting to know each other. She was asking me all sorts of questions, and one was about where Cameroon was in Africa. My father-in-law reached over to me, grabbed my arm, slid my sleeve up, and pointed at the location of Cameroon on my tattoo of Africa. Everyone started laughing, and it made me feel good because not only did he know I had tattoos, but he also knew where my Africa one was. Ha!

More breaking the mold, more bending from the norm. I still wore long sleeves after that anyway. *Respect is a long-distance run.*

As I said, I know I should be loved for who I am, and that's fine. I don't think I would have married the Korean if I had not been welcomed by his family like that because I have too much self-worth. I just wouldn't want my children to go through that. I do understand that others chose to love anyway, and I respect their choice. Same if he hadn't gotten along with my mother and brother. Love is one thing I insist upon in marriage. It was my deal-breaker, had anyone thought to ask.

I'm old-fashioned, I guess. I just don't need to start any new negative patterns. There are enough old ones to break. I don't want my children to feel anything but love and affection. I'm glad it came together the way it did.

I'm so grateful for my in-laws. They made such a wonderful son; they did such a good job with him. He's such a good man, and I would follow him anywhere. I would live with him in a room. I would live with him in a mansion. I would live with him in a shack.

Soon after, we celebrated the Korean's birthday, which falls a week after mine in Hong Kong. My sister Babs and her husband Vivek are huge foodies, and we had so many fantastic dinners. Oh, the food with Babs is legendary! I could write an entire dossier on her taste. Vivek, her husband, is from Bangalore, India. We adore him, and they have two daughters, Adele and Sophie.

Our whole family went to the Spring Moon restaurant at The Peninsula Hong Kong on the Korean's birthday. We went there by boat. We dined on the finest Peking duck. Peking duck is a dish from Beijing that has been prepared since its Imperial Era. It has a golden, delicate, crispy skin; it is actually almost *all* skin. You might complain there isn't enough meat, but traditionally that's how you eat it. You eat it with a bean paste, hoisin sauce, onions and cucumbers, and Chinese pancakes that hold all that goodness. There are special ducks just for this dish. They are washed inside out, glazed in syrup, roasted, and finally carved in front of you. You don't cut anything; it's sliced for you. The Chinese and duck are a thing of culinary beauty.

At that dinner, my sister told the Korean, "We are really excited to have you and welcome you into our family" and "...so glad to see how happy you make Africa." By then, I had dropped the Suzanne in my name and was known personally and professionally as simply Africa. She went on, "We fully expected her to someday retire from bachelor life in New York."

Vivek chimed in, "...and marry a man whose first name ended in O." They held up their champagne glasses. "Welcome to the family."

I was like, "Wait, what O?" I said, laughing at their comedic toast. This is why I love them, by the way; a hot mess of laughter, we always have it.

"Oh," he replied, "You know, Giancarlo or Roberto or Massimo, or something like that." He was referring to my Italian phase. We all cracked up laughing and my niece, who had been secretly reading a book under the table until then, asked me if I had had a boyfriend named Massimo before.

I said, "Probably, but I don't remember now."

That same year on Christmas night, a few months after returning from Seoul and Hong Kong, the Korean, who asked my mother and brother's permission in advance, proposed to me. Two days later, we were wed. We had another wedding in Cameroon a year later, but we married first alone. I wore a white vintage dress from a shop in Manhattan, and he wore a tuxedo.

My heart nearly exploded. I changed my name legally to Africa since I was taking the Korean's last name. To be Suzanne Yoon would be a total erasing of my Africaness by name. I could be anyone. Suzanne Yoon gave no clue of who I was. I like my African pride to shine from the moment someone interacts with me. Even if they choose to discriminate, I am okay with that. So, Suzy Africa became *Africa Yoon*.

Soon after that, the Korean got a job in Manhattan. We packed up again, keeping our Iowa place, and went to New York. Then three beautiful children came from our love shortly after our wedding in Cameroon. First came the twins Bijoo-Ruth and Hyung-Beau Dongshik, and my entire world changed. At my father-in-law's medical advice and personal thoughts, I also began to eat some meat and fish again. But I remained at almost 90 percent vegan, and now, I'm about 70 percent.

Then, extraordinarily soon after, when the twins were eight months old, I got pregnant with Baemin. In a short span of a few years, we went from being two strangers in Iowa to a family of five. He's the only man for me, truly: *for better or worse and richer and richer*, as we had edited our vows. He's the one. The end. The end of that part of the story, anyway.

11

There was magic, and there was madness. I was at the beginning of this split reality that was about to become my life. On day zero, before knowing, before the chaos and the wonderfulness of it all, I played with the children. It was one month after Baemin was born in fall 2017, and we decided to leave city life and moved to a large country house in Hackettstown, New Jersey, for a few reasons—one being we had finally left Iowa and brought our stuff east. We used to go back and forth a lot when it was just us, but we never went anymore with three children. So, while I was pregnant, we packed up our love space in Iowa and moved it east. We wanted to sort through it all, and we needed space to do that; an apartment or townhouse wasn't big enough.

I also wanted time to just focus on the children without the distraction of visitors every five minutes. Almost no one met the children as babies. Barbara, Vivek, and the girls flew in from Hong Kong. My sister-in-law was living with us for a time, and my mum also came. Much later, a handful of people met the children, but for the most part, I wanted no one. I can't explain it, but I just didn't want to be exhausted by visitors.

So, we moved into the house, but from Day 1, country relaxed living was not what we got at all. The Korean had to buy a bunch of space heaters because our big, beautiful country house we were renting wasn't well maintained, and it was the middle of winter. I remember when we went to see the house, the thermostat was at 62, and I said, "Oh, it'll be warmer than this, won't it?" The realtor looked at the landlord, who said, "Yes, yes, but we can't just run the heat high on a huge empty house; it's too expensive."

I was so tired, but I should have tested it out. Always listen to your instincts. But I was newly postpartum. I shouldn't have moved then, but after a week of it still not working, we tried to get out of the lease, but the landlord said he wouldn't give us back our massive deposit. My heart sank. *What choice did I just make?* I was so blissfully happy until then, but that was a major twist for a woman postpartum.

I dreamed of cozy nights in the country to recover from birth, but the furnace wasn't heating enough for us to be warm. Like a hero, the Korean figured out how to keep us warm.

It was on this night that I finally felt somewhat comfortable in my home. The baby was sleeping while the twins and I danced to Korean Pinkfong songs playing on a Bluetooth speaker. I was their only Korean teacher for now, teaching a language I don't even speak myself, and loving it. I was speaking in French, speaking Korean words, and it was my little heaven. The day was winding down, and we were in the kitchen when suddenly, this feeling came over me. It was like things weren't right in my body. Everything began to look blurry.

But I was so happy at that moment. Of all the things I've done in my life, being a mother just flowed. It's easy for me, and

I have so much energy stored in my body that even when I am tired, energy remains. What I was going through had nothing to do with stress as a parent or the burdens mothers take on raising their children. At the time, I had no idea what it was.

The only thing I could think to do was just crank the Pinkfong tunes louder and keep dancing. We were singing in Korean about a baby shark. A shark that would go on to become very famous, but at the time, it was just "agi sangaw doo doo doo doo doo." Yet, that feeling refused to go away. I couldn't just make it stop in my usual way. My legs began to feel very weak. I got the kids into a game, but I needed a break from dancing. That's when the house suddenly looked very smoky.

It wasn't a fire or anything burning in the oven. It was my vision. Stubborn, I called the Korean to ask him if there could be smoke with no fire. I was a bit scared, but I was trying to hold myself together.

He was on the train home from work in Manhattan and told me to hang in there. Even when my insides are screaming and my mind is racing, he has a way of calming the madness like a true hero. Just the sound of his voice can do it. With my heart beating excitedly and my blurry vision coming and going, I looked for anything to take my mind off of what I was going through. In my experience, doing that meant pouring myself into something else to keep myself going.

I went to the desk and wrote on a piece of paper, *What do you want?* At the time, I was working on our nonprofit called the K America Foundation, a program that spreads Korean culture using language, arts, and technology to fill kids with self-esteem and Korean pride. African Action on AIDS, my family's charity, is now a twenty-year-old charity that aids orphans in Africa who have lost their parents to this deadly disease. We get the kids to school and keep communities clean. With African Action on AIDS, my kids already had a program where they could give back to their African side, and my husband was involved too. What my children needed was a way to serve the public on their Korean side. That's what the K America Foundation set out to do.

But to get started, we needed a building. I started looking for buildings on the computer. Pouring my mind into that was how I was trying to find my escape. That was a coping mechanism I used a lot. I would tell myself that my heart was racing because I was excited about changing people's lives. "Yay!" I'm doing something great for people, and that's why my heart is beating out of my chest. I was fooling myself, and I fooled myself better than anyone else around me.

There was both magic and madness in all of this. I convinced myself that if my dream wasn't big enough, the madness would swallow me. But if my dream was huge, the magic would pull me through. I was trying to let the magic pull me through while looking for a building big enough to house my dream. It was about that time that the Korean came through the door and saved me.

He took over with the kids. The way I felt, I was glad he was there in case something went wrong with me. The kids were safe, and that was a huge relief. But it's more than that. We are so connected that he feels it when I'm down. He knows something isn't right. In our marriage, I'm a very traditional wife. Even though I'm an activist who gives a lot of my time to my charities and foundations, I do all the home stuff, too, just as I dreamed it. I cook and clean. I put out the Korean's clothes. I'm out of the 1950s, and his part is to take the trash out and fix things that break. It is a very old-school marriage arrangement, but we are happy, and it works for us. And that's the thing. I run the house. When the house runner is broken down, things get tough. He notices, or I remind him.

When he got home, I still pushed myself through the motions. When he took the twins up to bed, I went with him, and we went through our nighttime routine. We have a stars and moon machine that we put on when we turn off the lights. Then, we sing "stars and moon, stars and moon." But we sing it in Korean and in French. Then, we sing it in my mother's native tongue Basaa.

In Korean we sing, "tal tal tal, byeol byeol byeol." Then we sing in French, "lune lune lune, étoile étoile étoile." And then in Basaa, "song song song, chodot chodot chodot"

Tears were streaming down my face as we sang in the dark. My husband held me up as I was trembling, and we made sure that the kids could not see me. We took each of our children between us and hugged them. We gave them a million kisses. It's our whole routine before my husband prays in Korean. He prayed for me that night. He is my rock, but he was worried too.

After the prayer, he went to feed the baby. I thought a workout would make me feel better. I thought it might help get rid of the feeling that I never named anxiety. Our exercise equipment was set up in the mother-in-law suite on the other side of the house. It wasn't my best workout. I ran, and it did make me feel a little better. I was at least proud of myself for giving my spirit what it needed at the time.

As I walked back across this seemingly vast country home, the world turned completely upside down for me. The house felt like it was spinning, and I had to crawl up the steps. I have never been so scared in my entire life. I wanted to yell out for the Korean, but the kids' room was at the top of the stairs. I remember having the sense not to scream even though something inside of me was broken.

I crawled to our room. The entire way, I felt like I was going to die. My heart was racing, my arms were weak, and my legs felt like Jell-O. I got to the cold, icy room and looked up at the Korean. His name fell out of my mouth with tears and saliva pouring from my face. "I'm dying," I said.

He looked at me. "What's going on?" He's not a man of many words when connected with emotion, but he ran over and got me off the floor. I was trying to figure out what was going on and why I felt this way. But I couldn't. I didn't have the story, and I couldn't trick myself this time. It was serious. This wasn't something I could just explain away. We thought about calling an ambulance, and we kept going back and forth about it. I was trying to be strong and convince myself it wasn't that serious.

At six in the morning, we decided it was time to go to the ER. We didn't make a fuss about it. We got the kids up and played a happy game with them while we got them dressed. We made some superfood pouches and grabbed *gim*, a dried Korean seaweed snack, for them to eat while we were there, and we headed out the door.

The ER was empty, which is good to see when your heart is racing, and your body feels like it just wants to quit. The ER in this sleepy country town had a little room where he could take the kids to play. They watched Korean cartoon videos on his laptop.

As I approached the front desk, I suddenly burst out in tears uncontrollably. I told the nurse I wasn't feeling well and needed a doctor, which must have been hard to understand with me breaking down in front of her. But she knew what to do. She told me to take a seat while she informed the ER doctor that I was there.

As I sat waiting, my legs shaking and my body weak, sad thoughts started going through my mind. I remember thinking about how young my kids were. I just got them. My life was so great, and I was so happy. *What if I die? What will happen to them? What will I leave them?*

I decided that I needed to create a magical life for my kids to learn everything I valued. I had to leave them something majestic and purposeful to do. It was the worst feeling to think that I might die while my life was going so great and that this would be all there was to it.

I also thought that if I lived, I better get busy with my life. I knew I needed to share the same dream with my kids and teach them how to use their lives and who they were to serve. They are Cameroonian Korean Americans. I had the African side down. I wanted to make sure they also knew how to help their Korean selves.

I thought about that as the nurse put in the IV. I thought about that when they wheeled me to the MRI to check for blood clots. And I thought about that the whole time I was there, and my body was shaking. That's what scared me the most. This was something serious that positive thinking couldn't just think away.

"What? That can't be right." I was staring at the nurse, confused. What she was trying to tell me didn't add up at all.

Earlier that evening, I had felt horrible. My vision was blurry, and my heart was pounding out of my chest. I had fallen to the floor because something wasn't right in my head. I was a top, and the world was spinning beneath me. I had no idea why. I had to climb the stairs on my hands and knees with saliva dripping from my mouth and tears streaming from my eyes.

Was this nurse telling me I got my babies out of bed and rushed to the hospital for the flu? It was no flu! But that's what she insisted.

"You are displaying symptoms of the flu, ma'am," she said in a soft tone—the kind of soft tone that can drive me up a wall when I'm frustrated, and the answers don't make sense. They spoke in that soft tone to keep people from getting upset, but it made things worse because I felt like they weren't listening and weren't looking hard enough. I didn't feel the way I felt, uproot my children out of bed, and drag them to the hospital for the flu! Something wasn't adding up, and I knew it. I felt it. But they weren't listening.

***

The rain was falling hard as the ambulance pulled under the covered entrance and stopped at the sliding glass doors. The EMTs rushed me out on the gurney and pushed me into the ER, where the nurses were standing ready to pump me full of questions and drag me through a gauntlet of tests. I knew them by name now, and they certainly knew me because this had made my third visit to the ER since the first night when I felt like I was dying.

I still felt like I was dying, but they could never find anything wrong with me. First, they thought it was the flu. Then, they said it was a bug. I wondered what their reason was going to be this time, but it wasn't a bug. There was something else going on, and they just weren't looking deep enough. Black women spend more time in the ER convincing doctors we are in pain or distress than actually getting treated.

Nurse Carol, let's call her, looked at me with her arms crossed. "Did you take care of those babies?"

With half a smile and a voice out of breath, I answered, "Yes, I did. I tucked them in and kissed them goodnight before I just couldn't take it anymore."

She cocked her head and stared back at me. "Honey, you're going to be just fine. We're going to get you fixed right up."

They had my information, but they asked for it again. They wanted to know especially about why I would leave the comfort of home and get rushed there on a dark, rainy night just to hear a doctor tell me I have anxiety or something else that wasn't worthy of a trip to the hospital in the middle of the night. It wasn't anxiety. It wasn't the flu or a bug. It was something serious, and I knew it. I just couldn't get through to them. How were they missing it?

I took my smartphone and extra battery pack because I knew how this visit was going to go. Waiting for nurses to do their thing, I worked on my proposal for the K America Foundation. Waiting for a doctor to visit and tell me it was nothing, I sent emails to potential partners and grantmakers. I researched everything I possibly could to make sure the K America Foundation had a fighting chance from the get-go. I was scared; it was all I could do to busy myself.

In the back of my mind was a nagging feeling. My life was in their hands, and I was supposed to trust them. After all, they were the trained professionals who were supposed to know what to do. They went to school to study this stuff, right? But they weren't finding anything wrong with me. They kept trying to convince me that it was anxiety or a bug, and deep down, I knew better. After all, this wasn't my first postpartum rodeo. Although the twins were a straightforward pregnancy and delivery, I was diagnosed with a postpartum condition. However, I never experienced any symptoms that caused me discomfort.

The condition I had is not very common. It is easily missed, and you have to know to look for it. There is a gland shaped like a butterfly that sits at the base of your neck called your thyroid. When a person has postpartum thyroiditis, that thyroid gland can become inflamed at any time within the first year after giving birth.

It can last anywhere from a few weeks to eighteen months, and the symptoms are similar to what a mother goes through after childbirth. It doesn't show up until two months after the baby comes, so mothers sometimes are just fine and all of a sudden not so fine. Nurses and doctors can easily mistake the symptoms for the stress a new mother is under, including the psychological and physical pressures of postpartum mood disorders. The thyroid is supposed to go back to normal within a year to a year and a half, but there is a chance that postpartum thyroiditis could turn into permanent complications.

This butterfly-shaped gland is so fickle. It could strangle the breath out of me like a bowtie tightening around my neck, or it could one day fly away. Some days, it felt like just one butterfly made it hard for me to breathe, adding undue stress to my life. Then on other days, it felt like thousands of butterflies were choking the life out of me.

While working on my proposal in the ER, trying to keep my mind occupied, I waited for anyone to walk through the door. I didn't care who. Someone needed to hear me. I looked up as a nurse entered. Desperate to get someone in this hospital to start thinking anything other than this was a par-for-course case of a mother with a newborn baby, I asked again, "Could it be my thyroid?"

She looked at me and shook her head. "No. You're tired. It's normal."

I kept digging and asking questions. I had been through a fluctuating thyroid before but with no symptoms. I wondered if history was repeating except this time with the full monty of symptoms. My OB-GYN kept telling me that what I was feeling was normal and asked if I wanted pills to cope.

I felt so *used* by her. She was a doctor with a new practice. I felt like she just came, got the baby out, and she was done. She yanked my placenta out of me so hard I threw up. I don't know if it did or didn't have to be done that way, but it felt wrong. That's what I get for picking a doctor because she was next door to the pediatrician. Thank God for the two young nurses who were with me the whole time for Baemin's birth. It was the happiest experience; they were so amazing. We were singing and laughing.

After delivery, my OB-GYN was not much help when I called or even when I visited her for the follow-up. I never felt heard, but something was telling me it was my thyroid. I started googling it to find out more because I didn't know anything about it.

I had the symptoms. My heart was racing fast, and I was quickly losing weight, but everything else just kept coming back normal. My blood checked out. Nothing came up in other tests they ran earlier before the ER visits. Yet, I was still coming and going to the emergency room. Each time I went to the ER, it felt like I was going to die. Each time I went, they sent me away saying nothing was wrong with me but never checking my thyroid. It was an endless parade in and out of the ER. Me, knowing there was something seriously wrong and them telling me there wasn't.

"There is something wrong with me," I kept trying to convince them.

"Oh, you just have baby blues," they countered.

"No, there's something seriously wrong with me!"

"Oh, it's just anxiety."

Back and forth. Back and forth. That was until, finally, I had gotten tired of hearing there wasn't anything wrong with me. I knew my body. I had a gut feeling, and it's never been wrong about things. So, I had to yell at them to get their attention. "CHECK MY THYROID!"

I didn't say it like it was a suggestion. I was so scared that if they didn't acknowledge what I had been trying to tell them, that I could die, and they wouldn't be any wiser. They were stunned. I had never yelled at them before, but I had had enough.

Having grown up in the UN environment, I was programmed to do things to help people, to find effective ways that brought invaluable solutions to people's lives. That's why it was frustrating when I couldn't find a way to help myself. There's a duality that happens when you're having difficulties after you've had a baby. There are different emotions that women go through, that mothers go through.

On one side, you're ecstatically happy to have a healthy baby. For me, maybe because I had twins, and they had each other as a playmate, it made it much easier for me to focus on a newborn.

On the other side, it got hard for me when I became unwell. The worst part was the feeling in my gut that things were not okay. For most of my life, I've always been able to convince myself that the problems would be solved and the solutions would present themselves. It's an exercise I've always done in my mind to help me stay calm and rise above any situation. When something goes wrong, I talk myself through it, and a sense of peace settles inside me. I know everything is going to come out just fine and make the decision to take action.

This was the first time in my life that I believed in my gut that everything would not be okay. It was a different feeling. I even thought that maybe I wasn't going to live through this to survive what I was going through. It didn't matter if it was anxiety or hormones. It played havoc on me when I felt like my life could end.

There were times when I felt like I couldn't breathe. Frightening thoughts ran through my head. *Oh my God, I can't breathe. I'm going to die because I'm going to go out of breath.* It made me feel I was going to pass out and die. It was that serious.

Other times, I would get so dizzy. My head was not right at all. It's hard to concentrate being off-balance all day. It made me feel nauseous. It's hard to describe how frightening all this can be, but I didn't want to be scared. My rational mind tried to convince me not to be afraid. There was nothing to fear.

But for the symptoms, it was just another day shooting off warning signs. It had me wondering what was going on with my body? With my mind? I tried to step outside myself and observe what was going on from the outside looking in. But there were times when I didn't have the patience for all that. I just wanted to rip my shirt and bra off because I was straining to breathe. That's when it dawned on me. This was anxiety, wasn't it? It was. It had to be anxiety.

My heart rate would shoot up sky-high. Yes, anxiety makes your heart rate race, but it was ridiculously high. It was dangerously high, enough to scare anyone.

That's when I thought I was justified in going to the hospital. I thought maybe they were missing something, and instead of it being nothing or that I was possibly getting better, that it was getting worse, and I was going to die. The nurses rolled their eyes and gave me the same excuses to send me back home with nothing more than a helpless feeling in my gut. There was nothing more frustrating. I knew something was wrong, and the people I trusted to take care of me refused to look. I told them to check my thyroid several times. Then, I finally had to yell it because they just didn't want to listen.

That made me worry. They were missing it, and I was going through something serious. It wasn't in my head. If there wasn't anything wrong with me, why didn't I feel better? It was such a desperate feeling.

It always happened at night. I felt so alone even with people in the house. The feeling of desperation was terrible. It was not me. I just wanted to start feeling like me again and get better. I wanted to work out again. But some days, I just felt like I had lost myself. Thank God for my kids and the Korean because I thought maybe if I didn't have them, my mind would have gone.

I felt like I could have lost my mind over all this. I couldn't just let myself slip away to insanity, or my children wouldn't have a mother. They wouldn't have their mum. Especially my son, with my father having lost his mother during childbirth, I didn't want to repeat that pattern. *Is that my fate too?* I didn't want that again for him. So, I meditated and prayed. That's how I kept myself from losing my mind and my soul. I don't allow myself to get so scared and lost that I can't come back mentally or physically.

A couple of years ago, there was a story about a woman who dropped her kids off at daycare and was killed in a horrific train accident at the station. Years later, I found her husband and child. I couldn't help myself but tell him how sorry I felt for him. I told him to let me know if I could do anything. As a new mother, it made me think. Her child was a year old, and I was so heartbroken for him, but he was brave. We're friends on Facebook, and he is making this magical life for his daughter in Brazil.

I'm just so impressed with how he's dealing with the pain, and it makes me think. This guy had this horrible thing happen to him, and he's just carrying on, powering through with his daughter. He's so brave. I'm so impressed with his spirit. He's just in it, making that little girl smile. But I didn't want that for the Korean; all that work to find him to end like this.

The biggest fear for any mother is if something happened to us and our little kids don't have us anymore. That's how I feel about these symptoms, these butterflies. They call it having butterflies when you feel anxiety, like when you're nervous about something. Like my pauses before a speech or competing in a high-level race, you feel the butterflies, and they can help you, or they can hurt you.

It must be true because those butterflies in my neck, at the back of my throat, made me feel anxious too. Only this time, the pause before the speech takes too much time, and I never walk on stage because I am choking. There is no applause pause; instead, a thousand butterflies filled my throat like a death grip, and I died. It felt these were the last breaths of my life. I just wanted to live.

I wasn't feeling like everything was just going to work out. I couldn't just convince myself this time. It was the scariest thing for any person, but for a mother—and especially a mother of people who were just born and had just entered the world—it's a nightmare. The thing is, mothers don't always have time to stop everything and say, "Hey, this is scary. This is not going so well."

Mothers don't get that time because we are too busy thinking about our kids' childhoods, and we don't want it to be colored by anything negative. Whether it's illness or disagreement or financial lack or whatever it is. There were times when I would put my kids to bed, and then I would tell my husband to call 911 to have an ambulance come get me.

That's what it's like for a mother with little ones when you don't want to color their lives negatively in any way. We have to figure out how to convince our little sweethearts that everything is going to be okay, and even if you don't believe it, you have to find something that you can live for, which of course, is yourself. And because you live for yourself, your children will benefit from you doing so. You must have something that inspires and pushes you forward in the middle of that fear gripping you, something that moves you past that lonely thought that you're not going to continue here on this planet because there's a very good chance that you will.

"Check my thyroid!" It seemed to echo, and the doctor finally agreed. The nurses looked at me stunned, and then they nodded as they went off to run my thyroid levels. That's when they discovered it. The nurse came to me and exclaimed, "Oh my gosh. You have hyperthyroidism!"

I looked at her. "I told you. I knew it."

She looked at me and joked that my medical degree would be in the mail. Now that I knew, my tension was relieved a little, and I could joke with the nurse about it. A joke can be a joke, but there was something to be learned at that moment.

I think as women, we need to listen to ourselves. People just give us the runaround, and meanwhile, some real stuff is happening with us while they're trying to tell us something different, not taking us seriously. They aren't bad people. They're just operating in their field of understanding—what they have seen and their area of expertise.

An emergency room doctor or nurse just wants to make sure you are not dying. Even though you need more from them, it won't happen. Same for natural doctors who have a different perspective. They all answer you with what they know. Only you know the complete picture. This understanding is something that helps me heal much more effectively today. But this was my first major health crisis. All I knew was that my gut and instincts were telling me something wasn't right.

I had worked so hard to feel healthy. I want to wake up in the morning and feel amazing, not just okay. So, while doctors and nurses were telling me I had anxiety and the baby blues, which are real things, the fact is that what I was going through was something serious that they weren't finding. They weren't listening to me, and *we all deserve to be heard.*

I decided that I had to listen to myself. I knew something was happening, and I was right. Listen to yourself—and don't be afraid to speak up! It might just save your life one day.

It wasn't just the fact that I had to yell in the middle of the hospital for someone to finally hear me, with my voice echoing down the hall. It wasn't just that I had professionals around me who weren't listening to me when I talked. There was another factor, and it's frustrating, but it's very real.

I am not one to pull the race card. In fact, I'm the last one to do so. But if you asked, any black person could tell you about that feeling. It's a feeling we get when we know our race is a factor in the way someone is treating us. Thank God I have health insurance to keep doing checkups and a big mouth to keep pushing. Medical racism is real! I am very grateful to the doctors and nurses who were on my path, but the truth is a black woman in the current medical system can be treated very harshly. She has to speak so many times to be believed.

I find it alarming that black women are three and a half times more likely to die after childbirth. I had just had a child, and I had all these things worrying me. No wonder I was so pushy about my health. I have heard many stories, but most prominently was the story of Serena Williams.

She opened up about her childbirth, and it was shocking to hear that she had almost died after giving birth to her daughter Alexis Olympia. The first thing that went wrong was that the baby's heart rate dropped while Serena went through contractions. That resulted in an emergency C-section, which went smoothly. After the surgery, she felt a shortness of breath caused by a pulmonary embolism, which is clotting of blood in the arteries of the lungs. The coughing spell the embolism brought on caused her wounds to pop open, and she was rushed in for another emergency surgery. She said that her doctors were great, and the medical treatment she received saved her life, but women all over the world die from complications just like hers.

If she didn't advocate for herself, we could have lost a great woman, and so many have been lost. If they don't get the medical treatment they need, their child grows up without knowing their mother. Since black lives matter so little to people, these losses sometimes go unheard. *Little mama's bleeding. Mommy is gone. She slips away, but her life matters. Black mommy, you matter.*

I was aware of these facts, and this is what was in my head as I was dealing with doctors and nurses telling me I didn't have a problem. I knew my life was being threatened, and I needed serious attention. Medical issues worsen when someone who needs attention, as I did, is also dealing with medical racism. It can make something that could be treated early into a more significant problem because it is left so long. I felt the racism in the ambulances while I was being transported to the hospital. Sometimes, it would be me and a white man taking me with zero compassion, making me feel like I was crazy.

While trying to stay calm inside my head, I just wanted to scream. If I weren't carefully quiet and accidentally showed the nurses I was scared, if a tear came out of my eye because of how frightened I was, they would try to offer me drugs to sedate me. Sometimes I just wanted to cry, but I had to stay calm and say no to letting them sedate me with whatever. If I had a dollar for every pill they offered me, I would be rich.

Sometimes they would offer me strong pills, and then I would have to go home. I would shake my head like, *How does that work with me having to get myself home?* It was the middle of the night, and the Korean was with the kids. It was just us two, so I would take a taxi home. If I were drugged, that wouldn't have been very helpful to have me going home solo. *If I were sedated and trying to advocate for myself, who would have my back?* When he was able to be there, the Korean always had my back. He would notice things right away and say, "Hey, what? NO!" But as I said, many of these nights, I was alone, and he watched the children.

I went through different doctors and even changed hospitals when I was fighting for balance, the return to harmony just like the Korean lessons I learned through food. I had to for my health, my life, and my dignity. I needed someone who understood me, someone who sympathized with what I was going through, and who wanted to make sure I got through it. I was finally on my road to health when I arrived at a hospital, and an African nurse walked me in, then a young Indian lady attended to me. I had a Latina cardiologist check me out. When those women of color appeared, the healing began. We need more women of color in medicine, and we need them *fast*.

The country house was supposed to be a great time in our lives. It was the type of life we wanted. Sadly, that is not what happened. From heating the house with space heaters to those frightening moments at the hospital when no one was listening to me, it became a nightmare. The landlord was awful. If there is a book on terrible men, he would be in it. I believe it contributed to my health decline. He would call me nonstop. He was rude and had no respect for not only women but everyone in his way.

So, as I was going through hyperthyroidism, I had a reflection of chaos outside too. Don't move right after you have a baby in winter, no matter how perfect you think it'll be. Nevertheless, Mr. Rage Landlord, I thank you so much because you were the fire under my bum to get me to leave New York and New Jersey. I had never wanted to come back, but we had to sell my single-girl apartment, and we had our kids. It was all meant to be, and I will always love New York. But I used to get these visions that there would be a war or a pandemic in America. I told everyone, especially my mother, Bam Bam, Babs, and the Korean. We had to get out of New York. We just had to. What if there was a war or a pandemic?

I sounded a little crazy then, and many friends told me I was nuts. They would ask, when will that ever happen? *More postpartum anxiety,* I am sure they all thought. But now look at 2020-2021. The landlord in New Jersey pushed us out. Not literally, but spiritually just because he was unbearable, and then one day, the water heater burst and flooded the entire basement, ruining boxes of my work, and that was enough.

I just said, "Let's go." The Korean was working from home to care for me, and I couldn't appreciate more his boss allowing him to do that.

So just like when I found myself at a much younger age, overweight and tired, not knowing if I had anything left to give, change just wasn't going to happen on its own. If anything was going to happen, it was going to have to be me. Only this time, I had a family with me who deserved a good change as well. I was still in the middle of my thyroid flare-up, and a doctor had put me on meds, so my heart rate was semi-stable.

We were starting K America, and we put in a bid for a building in Minnesota. We had taken an RV to Minnesota to check it out. It was the perfect building that could be home for our work. We even liked the small town, and it was in the country.

Then one day, thousands of people were laid off at my husband's company, and the next week, they fired the company's CEO. My mother was visiting from Cameroon, and I was once again talking about my concerns regarding New York and New Jersey. After we prayed, I decided this flood in the basement was a sign from God. I got on Craigslist and picked a loft in Minneapolis. I did a Facetime tour with the kindest landlord, and we left the following week for Minnesota.

It was one of the best decisions of my life, listening to God and then letting Him move me on to the next place.

You have to keep yourself going somehow through the tough times. Mothers have to have a passion and a vision for their lives, which becomes the blueprint for how their children navigate the world by watching their *umma* live. Umma means mom in Korean. We have an essential and worthy role in raising the next generation. I know that living my life now, the way I believe we should, acknowledging our journey and the community at large, can be good for all of us.

It was now the summer of 2018. Baemin was eight months old, which meant the postpartum thyroid had anywhere between four and eight months left to end or rage on. The past year had been the craziest for me, the worst as far as my health goes. Creatively, however, it had been the best. I had heard the calling in the wind so clearly, and I had never been more inspired. As far as my goals, as far as my dreams, I took giant steps. Honestly, I think that's what kept me going. Whenever something good would propel me towards my goal, it would give me a boost. Life and living are the cure for everything.

I know that was a factor in fighting through all the issues I was having with my health. The things I was accomplishing boosted my spirits and helped me fight through it all. I'm not at the end of my journey yet. But I feel like that will pull me through always in my life—the pursuit of creativity and public service.

When I would reach out to somebody about being involved with my nonprofit, and they would get back to me, it made me feel like I was still alive rather than dying. It was something—

anything—to keep me going. It could be I felt good for only five minutes in my body, but in my mind, it felt like forever. I made excellent choices and was in deep joy.

When I got to Minneapolis in the fall of 2018, I hired a Tony Robbins business coach who told me not to strategize or do anything, unless I felt good. Even if I only felt good for five minutes, I would try to quickly figure out what I would do with those five minutes. I would make sure I accomplished something, even if it was the smallest thing, like writing emails. If someone replied and it was a good reply, it accomplished what it was supposed to do; it kept me going. That's what it was all about.

When an email would come back regarding a fundraiser, and they wanted to talk, I'd get on the phone with them. My heart rate would be 150 beats a minute, and I would be talking to someone about raising money for a nonprofit organization I was starting: "The K America Foundation to serve the Korean community, with special attention to Korean Adoptees." It is the biggest reason we picked Minnesota, as it's the home to 10,000 Korean adoptees.

My coach, Charlie, would boost me up so high, he would answer the phone during our sessions like he was talking to a superstar. "Is this the woman who moved her family to Minnesota with passion in her heart, the greatest giver alive?" he would shout. "FUCK YEAH, it is!" He was a former rock star, and yes, he cursed. I think he permitted me to as well. I needed his fierce "go get it" words.

When I went to the ER, I'd still find something to do while sitting there. He taught me techniques to keep myself in a state of bliss all the time, things I could do to call upon that energy. So, I would be in the ambulance going to the ER hearing Tony Robbins in my ears.

It was everything I needed. I am so grateful to that big man Tony Robbins; you have no idea! He got me out of a dark place. One day I'll thank him face-to-face for being my father from afar, both he and Pastor TD Jakes. They prayed over me through their work and uplifted me.

Never let yourself feel hopeless. Find something worth doing and work on it while you're going through the worst time of your life. Find the voice of someone out there who lifts you high when you can't. For me, it is my mother, the voice of Oprah Winfrey, Mr. Robbins, Bishop Jakes, and Nelson Mandela. That and the pansori songs of Korean culture and the sounds of haka, a tribal ceremonial dance of the Maori culture that reminds me of African drums. These pull me through instantly. Next time you need to summon courage, look up haka and watch a video, or go on YouTube and search *pansori Korean*. If you come out low, you didn't find the right stuff.

This is not a self-help book. I'm just telling my story about what I went through and that somehow an amazing life was happening parallel to my crazy health nightmare. It was the best year of my life and the worst year of my life.

The Korean did so much. He was still working from home, and my health wasn't getting better. I was up all night and then all day because he worked on the computer. Exhaustion was starting, but so was progress.

We had made an offer, using our personal savings, to buy that building in Northern Minnesota. There we would launch the K America Foundation. We thought it would be good to have a home base for the work, a place people could come. I had been writing the business plan in the emergency room in New Jersey. I finished it and submitted it to the city when we got to Minnesota. The offer was accepted. But because it was a government building, we had to present the business plan and then go through a series of hearings. We were putting ourselves out there on a limb. We risked it all. In fact, we risked more than uprooting ourselves and putting our personal money into a building we might not even get.

That and we faced some racism as we were buying the building. Some neighbors mentioned in a meeting that Asians brought diseases. At that time, it seemed like a minor hurdle, and the cause greater. We continued in spite and felt perhaps we needed to be there.

Everyone in the company where my husband worked was getting laid off. Everything was real. He was nursing me and protecting the children, and working a full-time job. It was hard. We were taking such a chance, and it was a scary time. He was allowed to work from home, and that was good. I was so grateful that his company allowed that because I needed him to be around.

He was so brave through all this. He deserves a medal. When things settle, I'm going to give him one. We realized we couldn't wait to see if he would be laid off too. We had to plan our future, especially with the new reality that I needed him to be by my side every minute. That had to end, though. I had to make a shift.

I started drinking some Korean postpartum soups, and I did acupuncture and took herbs. In the country in New Jersey, there was no Korean groceries or restaurants. But there were in Minnesota, so I was able to return to my regular health program.

12

I went extremely hypo in the next phase of the condition, and the doctors offered meds again. Only, this time treating me correctly. I have no problem with meds, but there has to be an actual reason. Not just, "Hello! Here are your meds," before I even talk. I took levothyroxine, and that helped me balance a lot. But more than meds, meditation helped me cope with stress.

I don't think you know if you have inner peace until you have some kind of bad thing happen, and then that's when you find out if you actually have inner peace. Before this, I was meditating, and I was so Zen, but I didn't have anything unbalancing me, like a health scare. It's when there is trouble you find out if you are peaceful or not. For me, to find out that I'm skilled at meditating did give me a lot of bliss. But I was not prepared for the rumble of what a health scare gives you.

That being said, if I didn't have meditation to calm me through this rumble I was going through, I might be in a straitjacket in some institution. This whole thing was already a mess, but it could have been a whole lot worse. I think meditation is the best armor for stress because I was fighting for that peace within.

You're like, "Peace within! I'm bloody well looking for you!" twice a day for twenty minutes. When you have health concerns, it's like that little taxi to inner peace becomes a rough ride. It's just like being in a cab in New York City that is taking you to JFK to catch a flight to Paris during rush hour. The freaking car came late, and you're sitting five minutes from JFK. You can see the airport. It's like you can reach out and touch it, but you're not moving. Anyone who's ever been to JFK during rush hour in Manhattan, you know what I'm talking about.

The taxi ride, though bumpy, still gets you there. When you have a whole world of things to worry about, when you have serious medical issues and babies to think about, that's what trying to meditate and finding your inner peace is like.

That's what meditating during this stressful time was like for me. I had to reach for it. I had to get to the gate. I had to get where I was going, except where I was going was not someplace or some meeting. I'm racing. I'm struggling. I'm pushing. I'm committed to my inner peace, to myself going to that place inside where a hundred million percent, there is peace no matter what. Not a perfect life but unshakeable peace to handle it; it's there every time and even to get five seconds of it is worth the trip. It's worth closing my eyes. It's so worth it.

It was worth it some days, even when I only found it for just a little bit before my condition yanked me back out of it. At least, I still found my inner peace that day. I am very grateful for Transcendental Meditation and for that time in Iowa. I'm thankful for the day that I learned about it and decided that I would learn TM. I'm very grateful indeed!

I looked forward to a time when it would not be such a daunting task to find peace within. It's a real thing. It does exist. And women are going through so much in search of peace. I believe that is how the world was created: In the search for feminine peace, God made our world. *It takes time. It takes time. Be easy. It takes time.*

Good stress is something that I've been thinking a lot about throughout this process. A lot of good things happened. The thing is that good stress still stresses out your body. Does your body know the difference between "My boyfriend is being such a jerk, he's driving me nuts. We've been fighting all night, and I haven't slept in a week," and "My boyfriend is so awesome, we've been talking all night on the phone, and I haven't slept in a week?" *Does the body just register unrest most?* I just wonder how your body knows how to deal with good stress versus bad stress.

Sometimes, it's hard to grasp. I was just a single girl five years before this with no husband and no kids, right? How fast we slide. I was super healthy, super happy, and super self-loving. I had just moved to Fairfield to work on dance, and then I met my husband. I didn't mention this, but while in Iowa, I created a show called *Inside American Fitness* for PBS. The new director for IOWA PBS and I moved there at the same time, him from L.A. and me from New York. So, I got a TV show and a husband. All good, right? Although it's all good, I believe all of it was still stressful for my mind and body—the sheer capacity of my ability to accomplish and realize my dreams.

That's the good stress I'm talking about. These were all good things. Getting married and moving back to New York is good stress because my life was moving forward in a positive direction. *What's bad about these things?* Moving, the physical and mental activity of it, even though I have very few possessions, is also stressful on your body, and yet, it was a good thing.

After we moved to New York, we started thinking about family. We were already planning a small wedding in South Korea. Just a small one. Nothing major. Then for fun, I'm producing a TV show and going back and forth, flying to Iowa. We were shooting in New York, Iowa, New York, Iowa. All good, right? It takes a lot of energy, and it's all positive, but it's all pretty stressful. And then the Korean looked at me like, "Hey Mrs.-Has-to-Get-Everything-Done-Right-Now, why don't we have a baby?"

So, we were trying to have a baby. Anyone who has had a child knows that it's probably best for life to calm down first. We shouldn't have been trying to do it while I was still producing a TV show. It was challenging. We were trying, and the baby wasn't coming. I wasn't bugging about it, but I started to realize that it wasn't as easy as one, two, three. I suggested that we get checked out to make sure we were all good. They could check out my eggs and check the Korean's sperm.

We checked out okay, but that put us in line where we needed to be. It put us on the road to understanding our bodies' timing. That's when it happened with guidance. BOOM! I was pregnant with twins! So, so, *so* good, right? Man, am I effective!

180

We planned on one and here, there are two of them in my body. It's a good thing. It's twice as good. But it's also more stressful for my body.

While I was pregnant, my dog of twelve years passed away. The love of my life left me, but I didn't have time to be depressed. I stuffed that away. I had two babies to think about. I don't know if I ever really grieved over him. I haven't had time to process it fully. But when the twins came, I couldn't have been happier. I wanted to keep going. At the time, I was thirty-eight. I wanted to have another child before I was forty. We tried again, and I got pregnant again with twins, but only beautiful Baemin made it. Half of my pregnancy terminated, and it was hard on me—the end of the good stress and hello to the bad stress.

Is there a difference in your body? Your body is probably just thinking, *Whatever you are doing, please, sit the fuck down.* Ha! See? Charlie taught me it's okay to curse sometimes.

So, then there was Baemin, my little fighter baby. She was like, "I'm coming. I'm in the world. I'm here." But I had a low-lying placenta, which means I wasn't supposed to do any crazy exercises or anything like that because it's dangerous. The problem is I had it all through my pregnancy. Even though I worked out every single day during my first pregnancy, lifting weights and running on the treadmill early in the morning and late at night, I wasn't able to move during this pregnancy. On top of that, I was still dealing with the loss. I was trying to be happy and grateful for the fact that I was having a baby.

When we finally decided that we would move our stuff out of Iowa and into the country house in New Jersey, it was right when I got pregnant. While it was all good, it was also stressful for my body. I never really rested well. Part of it would be exhaustion from all the good things that happened to me over those five years. I know I've covered the same ground, and it sounds like we went back and forth, back and forth between Iowa and New Jersey. That's not the case. Those are just separate layers of the same move from Iowa to New Jersey.

I mean, so much good happened that I don't even want to go over every loss. Don't get me wrong, losing a baby and a dog is very significant. But not as massive as to how many amazing things happened to me in those same five years. My life is just blessed with good stress. Lucky me.

Two months after Beamin came, I went through postpartum thyroiditis again. A lot of good things can happen, but good stress is still stress. If you're living a good life, you still have to be mindful that there may be some stress on your body that you're not recording on your list because you think stress is about losing a job or losing a dog. Good stress is still stress, *even if you're managing it.*

The medications finally worked for once, but there were other side effects. When I got to Minneapolis, I even started a workout program. The one thing I missed the most to deal with stress was exercise. While I wasn't sleeping, I would order exercise equipment. The Korean told me to stop that. It was good for me to keep hope, but expensive to buy all that stuff.

By the end of August, my blood tests were normal. We were about to go to Korea in September. I had never looked more forward to a trip in my life, and with the meds working, I thought, *Great! I can go!* A week before the trip, I drove for the first time to a hair-braiding shop to make an appointment to get my hair braided and buy hair. Then, I started feeling a thumping in my chest like I would have a heart attack. I had no choice. I had to drive home as quickly as I could. How could this be? I thought it was over, but it felt like when I was hyper again. I called the endocrinologist in New Jersey, and he told me to come off the drug and test my blood. My blood was normal, but I felt hyper again. I switched to a local endocrinologist who pumped me full of heart-slowing meds, so much so that my heart rate was too slow. The day we were to go to Korea, I slid out of bed like a puddle of water. The trip was canceled.

I went online to a Korean mommies group that I had joined on Facebook. The ladies cheered me up. They boosted me up so high; I will never forget it. Lots of praying, private messages, and people were sending me their phone numbers if I wanted to pray or talk. I got the airline to let me push the trip back, and by then, the Minnesota winter was approaching.

13

We were in Minnesota in the middle of the winter in negative 20-degree weather, which the weatherman would say feels like -51 or some insanely cold temperature, which was not helping me, even though I wasn't going out into the weather much. I was just in my loft, but the cold was not helpful. It wasn't conducive to my healing. Going to the emergency room wasn't conducive to my recovery. I was exposing myself to new germs, and then I caught strep at the hospital. Also, I had no idea that the lack of sun exposure began to tank my vitamin D levels. I never knew this or that black people need more vitamin D than everyone else.

So now I had strep for the first time in my life. Where else would I have caught it? I wasn't going anywhere except the hospital. I wasn't doing anything. Slowly I realized that I had a host of symptoms. They kept saying my thyroid was normal. Or that I had anxiety or other illnesses. Lo and behold, they were right for once. This time it seemed natural that the stress, both good and bad, had finally caught up with me. Throughout my pregnancies, I had stayed in touch with an old friend of mine from New York in my twenties; her name was Monica Gambee. Monica was extremely helpful to me, but the most important thing she told me was, "If you need help, get help. Don't act like some hero that has to conquer everything. Promise me if you need help, you'll get it." Every day I would ask myself that, even on the good days, and one day the answer became yes. I was scared to leave the house, and I hired some young Korean international students and Korean American girls to help me. But even when they came, I couldn't sleep. It was getting unbearable.

I wasn't sleeping because I was afraid I would die. That spot in my mind where I stayed positive was dimming. My Tony Robbins coach talked to me about therapy because he was a recovered addict. I thought, *I trust him, and that's what I'll do. I'll get help.* Therapy helped me out of depression, so maybe it could get me out of this too? So, when the insurance confirmed they would cover the sessions, I got on the phone to make an appointment. Then, I stopped. *Wait a minute! How am I going to do that? How am I going to go to therapy when I'm scared to go outside?*

At this time, the Korean, God bless him, was figuring out how to get our groceries delivered. When he would leave, I was a wreck. I didn't want to be alone with my kids. *What if something happened to me and they needed me?* I was so super grateful to his company that they let him keep working from home through all this. I was not well. But something was keeping me from healing, and that thing was sleep.

So, I started to think about my health the same way I did when my goal was to get married and have a family. Here I was again craving to be healthy—I had the family now, but I just wanted to enjoy them. Once I gained that awareness and realized a big chunk of what remained was anxiousness and lack of rest, I was a little ashamed that I was dealing with anxiety.

When I realized that's what it was, I knew I had to get help for that. I did not take the insurance-appointed therapist. I paid out of pocket for a therapist I found on my own online the day I admitted to myself that I had actually lost my mind. In therapy was where I just spilled it all out and worked through these issues. I did it on the phone twice a week, in my bathroom, and I had a great therapist.

He never told me, but I googled him one time and found out he was also a pastor, which was important because we started to talk about death. We would talk about things from a spiritual perspective too. It wasn't just about my physical issues, like why I couldn't get any sleep, but he started diving deep to find out what was *really* going on with me. He was a great partner to heal my soul, and I did the work on myself again.

It was like this magical thing he was doing because he gave me exercises, and we would talk about things on such deep levels in therapy; it was all starting to work. One night, I finally got some sleep. When I woke up, I shouted, "Wait! I just woke up. Does that mean I fell asleep?"

The sleepy but happy Korean said, "Yes."

I slept the next night and the night after that. I bought this gallon water bottle, and I drank it like water was ending on Earth tomorrow. What remained was strep, fatigue, and anxiety. I switched doctors again, and the new crew told me I was so healthy and to get off the meds that were dragging me down. The therapy worked. I will always be grateful to Vince Urquhart. He saved my mind. Goal-oriented therapy is wonderful. For a second time, I had set out to find my loves. This time I didn't have to run from New York to Chicago, though: they were right in my house.

One thing was that I belonged to that Korean mommies group, and they helped me out in so many ways. They prayed for me again once I announced that I was starting therapy, and they encouraged me. They had this beautiful, amazing energy that I had been missing in my life for so long, but I was starting to get it back.

I opened up to the idea of friendship again because those women showed me what it looked like, even online. Plus, memories of the Korean halmoni flooded into my head again. It must have been something about the Korean mothers talking about their mothers and their grandmothers that triggered something within me, but I remembered the Korean halmoni who had taught me so much so long ago.

I decided to start cooking for myself again because I had let that go for a few weeks. I was so wiped out. We were just ordering food to make it easy, but I wanted to start cooking my Korean food again. I had to get back into that.

I started watching the Marja Vongerichten show *Kimchi Chronicles* again, and the fact that she was a black and Korean adoptee was so fitting with where I was in my work. She and her husband Jean-Georges took such a deep dive into Korean food from flavor to story.

I began by re-watching my favorite episode, *The Seafood Chronicles*, which sees them travel to Jeju Island in Korea. The episode starts with Chef Jean-Georges going diving for the fish with a chef friend and the famous *haenyo,* who are freediving female sea farmers of the island. All this while Marja and her daughter have a spa day. When the fishing ends, the haenyo make the men a *haemul jeongol* from all they caught in the ocean. Jeongol is different from the typical stew that people are more familiar with, which is called jjigae. The only simple way I can explain it is that a jeongol just tends to have more in it. Also, the ingredients tend to be spread out in a wide shallow pot.

The episode then continues back in their kitchen in New York, and they begin to make their own haemul jeongol and my favorite miyeok-guk. To watch such accomplished chefs handle the dish and make it their own inspired me. I asked the Korean to go get me all the seafood he could find, and now that I was eating meat and fish again, I was excited to try the dishes. I made the miyeok with mussels and then made my own mélange of seafood to make the jeongol. I used mussels, squid, shrimp, crab, napa cabbage, Korean radish, some carrots, mushrooms (I had dried ones, which I added to water while the Korean was out shopping, but he brought back enoki mushrooms too), and scallions.

The sauce had gochujang, gochugaru, ginger, and always too much garlic. I added a little doenjang, fish sauce, used an anchovy broth, and more that I don't remember. They had lobster; I did not, but I was just trying to mirror their style of a little this and taste and a little that and taste as I went along. As I watched and cooked, Marja was saying that Korean food was not so precise, and that encouraged me to find my own flavor. I remember putting out the food on our table. I put out banchan I made, and we ate so well that night.

The children love miyeok gook too, especially Bijoo (she might love it more than me). I cried after I made that meal because it felt so good, and it made me feel alive and encouraged. The Korean was so happy. That night, I said a prayer of thanks for the Vongerichten family. They had reignited my passion for Korean food, this time with seafood.

I wanted to watch more and learn more. I was possessed once again; my attention toward living began to drown unwellness completely. I posted food in the Korean mommies group, and one of the moms turned me on to a woman named Maangchi on YouTube who made many Korean dishes.

She was lovely. "Hello, everybody," she greets at the beginning of her episodes. My children were always saying, "Hello, everybody!" They were so little, but I played her on a large screen. These people began to become a huge part of our family. Korean chefs like David Chang and Roy Choi became my inspiration points; it was interesting to watch how people were making the food their own. It made me want to make my own styles as well. I also began to follow a young man named Chef Chris Cho, who is a son of Korean chefs in Philadelphia.

I found him randomly, and he made me laugh so much with his videos.

I found his account one night while I was in the ER, and he made me laugh so loud when he yelled, "Ooh!" and "Yobuseyooo!" And everything was Philly slang, so "jawn" this and "jawn" that. I had just finished telling the doctors that I thought I was dying, and then there I was laughing so loud at this guy.

"You're laughing so much," the doctor said. "So, are you feeling better?"

I said, "In my head, yes. Keep checking the rest of my body."

It was a different time with the internet. Instagram was very popular and so much more was at my disposal. The Korean bloggers, Korean chefs, my mother-in-law's recipes, and the Korean mothers pulled me back to cooking Korean food every single day of the week. Every meal was Korean, but now that I wasn't vegan, I dove deeper into it, including all the meats and seafood.

The two Korean girls helping me with the children were like, "Whoa! You cook like in Korea," when I would serve them dinner or lunch.

I posted recipes and the plates I was doing in the Korean mommies group. I was making so many banchan now—so many. Even the mothers were amazed. I got comments like, "Wow! That looks like Mother's. You really know how to cook."

All this positive energy boosted me, and the whole family was eating right. I not only wanted to feed my kids Korean food because it was their culture, but the Korean loved that I was back to making Korean food as I had before, just on another level. It was a deep, deep dive back into love for us after such hard times. Every soup I made, every mandu I folded gave him much comfort. He really deserved it after all he had done. Mostly, though, I made Korean food for me, for my healing, for my soul. I was inspired again.

Between returning to Korean food and going to therapy, sleeping, and drinking lots of water, I started feeling much better. When I went to the doctor to scan my thyroid, there were no more nodules, and I had been off the meds. Korean food is my love, and I will cherish and celebrate it until the day I die.

Korea started beckoning me. I wanted to heal more. I yearned to have access to all the Korean ingredients and healing foods. I wanted to go to Korea. The time was near when we had pushed back our tickets from the canceled September trip the year before. It was March 2019, and we had to book a trip now or lose the money.

A whisper came to me one day. I had to listen. I looked at the Korean and just said, "Let's go to Korea. Let's just go!"

We were in a month-to-month lease for our loft in Minnesota because we came sight unseen, and I wanted an out just in case it didn't work out. Also, Minneapolis wasn't where we would stay full-time. It was temporary to connect to the work we would do there and buy the building, but we always wanted to live in many places. We just hadn't figured out exactly where because of what I went through. I was feeling good and wanted to live then and now.

The kind landlord returned our deposit. As I thought about all this, it just seemed too easy of a decision when I started asking the Korean, "We don't have to stay. We only have to give notice, right? We can technically leave here. Let's get rid of our apartment, and let's pay rent in Korea. Let's go to Korea. I want to be in Korea. I want to be surrounded by every possible healing ingredient. I want to immerse myself completely. I want to go to the Korean spa. I want to eat Korean food. I want to drink Korean tea. I want to be immersed as I have never been immersed in Korean health culture before. I want my kids to see their grandparents and Korea. I want to learn more about Korean culture to guide our foundation's work and let the Korean government know about our work. Every single part. Professionally. Family. Spiritually. Medically. Korea is calling me."

It just made sense for my being and my world. My husband took one look at the ticket and said, "Well, for how long?"

"Book a ridiculously long return date in the fall, and we will figure it out."

He took a few deep breaths and said, "Yep! Let's do it."

"We always said we were going to live in all these different places," I said to him. "That we were going to live in Minnesota and Hawaii, and we were going to spend time in L.A., then Korea and Cameroon too. We wanted to be global always, right? Why are we waiting? You never know what happens. We wanted our kids to go to Korea since they were born and feel connected to it. So, let's do it."

I think he thought it was crazy, but he said, "Yes."

When I started healing, I was so grateful for everything. I mean, I always heard those stories of deathly ill people when they finally grasp the meaning of life. They're so close to death, and at that moment, they realize everything about life. They remember the smell of a flower. They remember their children, their mom, their father. Being so close to death makes them finally appreciate what life is all about.

I've always been a grateful person before I wasn't well, but if you go through anything that makes you wonder about death and it doesn't change you, it was a waste. You can't experience this whole huge episode in your life and come out on the other side, not being even more grateful when so many others don't recover. In my Korean moms' group, I have learned too much about motherhood and life.

I recently lost a dear Korean mommy friend from another mommy cooking group; God rest her soul. She found out she had leukemia, and then she passed away three weeks later. I remember I had just messaged with her. Stuff like that hits hard, but it also makes me reflect.

When something happens, and you survive, it should make you want to *truly* live. I evaluated everything around me and everything that was a part of me. I realized how I used my toes when I walked. I noticed how I used my heels when I ran. I saw my breath hit the top of my lip and warm it.

Before leaving for Korea, the K America Foundation hosted its first event. I was the host of a special event that we called Hanbok Walk. *Hanbok* is the traditional attire of Korean culture. We were having a walkathon in a park to celebrate that beautiful national dress of Korea and celebrate Korean adoptees and their stories. My healing was a bit new at the time. I was worried that I wouldn't get through this event or even talk because I was hosting it.

What got me through was that lots of Korean adoptees had been coming to my house for dinner, and they were telling me their stories of the things they had been through as adoptees. It was humbling me even further and making me even more grateful for my life. So, I was just in this deep state of gratitude, and I was writing about it in my journal. I was going through a journal a minute. There weren't enough pages!

We connected with a young man named Wayne Kangas. He touched our hearts so deeply and became a little brother we never knew we needed. He grew up in Minnesota, and he gave us a deeper understanding of the Korean adoptee experience. Having him over for supper became something that lifted my spirit, and seeing him with my husband in brotherhood filled my heart with joy. It's like they were related; they acted so alike. They watched Korean movies and played with the kids. Wayne is a magic guy who the world should watch.

So, with all this, I was lifted by God, and I not only could host, but I enjoyed this event. These adoptees, too, gave me the spirit, and I was able to get through because of what they had been through. Also, I didn't want to miss anymore, and I began to exist and live. Not because I was dying, but because I was grateful to be alive.

As we packed, I thought about how the Korean also went through so much, bless his soul. We also did some couples therapy to protect our love, but I'm now working on slowly healing him, too, because what we went through was hard. He had no instruction manual, and he had no idea what it was like to care for someone who was that anxious. He deserves more than a medal for fumbling through the best he could. Someone ought to give credit to caregivers because there is a lot of work to do when you get sick. As in his Korean nature, he's not always good at expressing emotion, which can come off as cold. When you're anxious, it feels mean, even when you understand the culture like me. Mostly he said nothing at times because he didn't know what to say. I am grateful for him, and it isn't just because he showed me how much he loves me by always being there and saying sorry when he felt he made mistakes. He is a real man and a terrific father. It went from me doing all the house and baby stuff while he was working to jumping right in and taking over.

He's my hero and the love I always sought, even more after he stood by me sick like that. I'll never forget. I forgive myself and him for the times we were mean to each other. Some old patterns came out of me, and therapy helped, but I wasn't a great person to care for sometimes. I apologized, and he apologized, but at some points, that did not help. So, when we needed help, we got it. My older sister Pamela came, and my sister Teresa also came during challenging moments. I think that loyalty healed me a great deal. I called Teresa from the hospital one day, and the following morning there she was. Also, the night I finally slept, Pamela made me African food. It was some good, heavy fall asleep African food too. Maybe I didn't need therapy. Perhaps I just needed *garri*, a heavy rolled ball made by mixing a cassava powder with water, to get me to sleep! Africans will laugh about that one.

So, we got through, the Korean and me, still committed as ever, still searching for complete healing and our dream. We took this massive action and packed our whole family, and headed for Busan, South Korea.

14

Once we booked our airfare and found an apartment, I can't even begin to tell you the level of joy I experienced. I was like a little kid, so excited like I had never gone on a trip before. I mean, I've been traveling since I was a child. I traveled around the world alone when I was nine years old! Travel was nothing new to me, but this trip was different.

When we got on the plane, and I sat in my seat, I was talking in both English and broken Korean about how we were going to Korea. I was literally in tears. They were just flowing down my face. When that plane took off, so did my spirit. It was like I was going home, and I'm not even Korean. I think it was all the immersion that I had been doing up to this point. It started to make me feel like going to Korea was going home.

I've only had that feeling about going to Cameroon, my own country. Even my kids felt it, and my husband did too. We were just thrilled, and it was such a long trip. Can you imagine with three toddlers? It was such a big trip, but my kids did so well. They slept most of the time, and even when they were awake, they were remarkable for three little people under the age of three. My hat goes off to them for being such little wonderful grateful beings. Eating Korean food on the plane was pushing me forward, and my kids ate the kimchi. The hostesses were so impressed that they were eating kimchi and calling it by name.

I smiled, watching them talk to the children in Korean and eating my side of Korean radish.

Instead of aggravating everyone and draining everyone of all their energy, they were making everybody happy. Also, they get a lot of attention. They're basically like celebrities. Traveling with them is like traveling with Beyonce. Korean people were super into my kids. It was like traveling and experiencing fame. People wanted to take photos. People wanted to greet them. People were just interested in them. They have this magnetism, and it was all very positive. For me to have this positive welcome of my family, it's on the backs of all those who had experienced so much pain before, and I thank them with gratitude.

I had to start a hashtag #famousinkorea for my Facebook because of all the people fawning over my kids and all the photos they took. It wasn't just on the plane. It was at the airport too. People were coming up to us and saying how cute they were and how gorgeous they were, asking for photos, and some girls even screaming as if we were the black Beatles. If my kids even uttered one Korean word, people just fell over it. There were so many high-pitched Korean sounds coming our way. *KEE-AHH WOOOH*, which means cute, if my kids giggled or even breathed. They were eating it up.

We stayed at a hotel the first night to rest and recover from the long flight before going to Busan. It was a very magical day for my whole family. We had so much fun in that hotel. The kids were delighted. All of the Korean cartoons that I would look for online were on the TV when we turned it on. My kids were amazed, "What is this TV that has all of our favorite shows that we watch all the time?"

We ran around the massive hotel in Incheon. We played hide-and-seek. We were all two-year-olds that day. The Korean planned it all. I kept putting my hand on his cheek and saying, "Thank you, *yeobo*," which means honey or sweetheart. He made everything from our arrival on wonderful. That is who he is. He's the story under the story—the story that allows the story to *be*.

We got off the train that we had taken from Seoul to Busan. We were in a taxi, and it was at this moment when we were crossing the Gwangandaegyo Bridge, the sun beamed through the window and shined on my face. That's when I felt this deep feeling in my soul that I was home.

I didn't understand it entirely. I mean, how could I feel like this about a place that I had never been to before? I thought about that Korean halmoni and wondered what she would think of me in her country. I thought about my mother, who was so happy for me to be out of bed finally. And I thought about myself and everything that I had been through.

It's a testament that if you believe in your spirit and take massive actions, you can get anywhere you want to go. You have to truly believe it, though, because I saw Busan in my mind. I had pictures of Busan. I had written about Busan. I had read about the film festival in Busan, and I had read about the fish in

Busan, the second-largest city and most famous beach town in Korea, Haeundae, where we would live.

Now, here I was. We got into our apartment, this tiny apartment. I've never been in an apartment so small, but I didn't care. It could have been one small room with only a chair, and I would have been just so happy and grateful to be there.

My soul was finally at ease. I was used to checking my heart monitor five or six times a day, and I hadn't checked it once. That's how at peace I was.

I slept so well that I woke up at five in the morning. I went outside and ran on the beach. I did that for two days before I decided to change things up and hike up a set of stairs I found on the edge of the beach. They lead to a trail and a beautiful bridge. When I got to the top of the stairs, a group of Korean grandmothers, who reminded me of the Korean halmoni back in Jersey, were exercising. One of them saw me and motioned for me to join in. Just like that, I started doing their program.

It was this beautiful Korean movement program that these grandmothers do every morning at 6 a.m., and they invited me to keep coming. So, every morning, I would go for a run from five to six, and then from six to seven, I would do this movement stretching. It was unique. They yell out to the ocean, and there I was again, this black girl with these Korean grandmothers. We got so friendly that sometimes their feet would hurt, and I would massage their feet mid-workout.

They reminded me so much of the Korean halmoni from the market who disappeared on me. It was like Halmoni had returned but multiplied.

I took selfies with them because I didn't do that with the Korean halmoni from Jersey. I made sure I was going to get something to remember all these grandmothers by. They were so warm; it became the highlight of my trip. It was the best. It was the spring of April 2019, and the winter of my illness was melting. My diet mainly consisted of fresh Korean vegetables and banchan again, but this time fish, so much fish, every day. I joined a gym, and my gym membership came with a membership to a Korean spa, and there I was again, just like I was back in Jersey: the only black girl with all the Korean ladies.

Leaving Minnesota, I felt better. But in Korea, I was healing myself. Coming out of what I had gone through, every layer that peeled away felt better. I had no way of knowing the depth of my recovery because it all was better. But this healing, the Korean healing, I knew it would be complete.

The one part of my diet I really love is all the kimchi. I already had a love for kimchi from when I first started eating it years before, but I was tasting the local kimchi. Every region in Korea makes kimchi so different. I was eating so many different kinds I had never even tried before. The kimchi became life to me. I was eating and healing, moving and sleeping, dipping my body in the ocean, and walking. I went to the grocery store. It was not packed with shoppers or busy. A wonderful older lady walked me around and gave me all the ingredients to make kimchi. But because we were in Busan, the local seafood ingredients were different. She had me tasting all this kimchi; it was a wonderland of flavor. That day, the Halmoni was so fresh in my mind. I recognized that her behavior and kindness were like the woman in this store sharing her culture. I hoped I could give that as a gift myself someday.

The change of time zones worked in my favor as I was sleeping very well, and then, every day, I was out in the sun. I was getting so much sun, and that is such a good part of healing because I was getting all that vitamin D. The stage was set for me to heal, and I knew that I would be okay. I had been through so much, and the only confidence I would have that I was well again was to feel better for a long while. It was the summer of 2019 that I started believing that I was, in fact, in a much better place health-wise.

It was amazing. I took my kids to Korean kid cafes designed for parents to get a little bit of a break. I worked on my foundation from these Korean kids cafes while other people watched my kids and played with them. I actually got my work done, like writing letters to the government and planning new programs. There, I came up with a Drama Therapy program, which leveraged my time at NYU studying acting to be used as a tool for adoptees to release their emotions. I found out what I wrote in Busan had a medical basis as well. I was excited to implement it, and I continued to write each day.

We were in Busan only a few weeks into our trip when my mother-in-law came down from Seoul, and I was so happy to see her with our children. She was so joking and loving with them and feeding them nonstop. Although they live so far apart, all the truths about grandmothers take instant effect. She noticed already what they like to eat. When they would cry, she would hold them. It was like she already knew them so well. She took them to eat *jjajangmyeon,* the children's favorite dish in Korea. It was the Korean's favorite childhood dish in Korea as well.

Jjajangmyeon is a Chinese-influenced Korean noodle dish. The noodles are topped with thick black bean sauce that has chopped vegetables (in Busan, there is seafood in it) and topped with cold cucumber slivers. You toss the sauce into the noodles and muddle through the delicious paste that takes over your entire existence, including trying to keep it off your clothes. Here's a tip: lean forward. But for children, their faces are instantly covered with black bean sauce. They love it, and she loved giving it to them, buying it for them, and telling me the best way to make it.

She helped correct my Korean on documents for work. She was so good at it that when people called me back to follow up with me, they would speak to me in Korean even though my Korean was not that great. She made me look so good. She's just such a wonderful woman. We also spent time with my father-in-law, and he said the children were well behaved (he said more than that, but that made me the happiest).

I completely immersed myself in the culture, and especially with the Korean grandmothers. It was an amazing time. After running, I would take the children for long walks on the beach; my kids were having their photos taken all day. I can't even begin to explain to you just how many photos people wanted to take while we walked on the beach. We were surrounded by people taking photos and telling us how beautiful we were.

I would say thank you every time they approached. Remembering the history of Korea, I would thank God aloud. I did not complain about the attention because I knew that the flash of the camera taking a picture used to be stones and cigarettes thrown at people like us. I could take a little flash. In twenty years, another family might walk down the street, and there wouldn't even be pictures taken, just considered normal Koreans. So, I welcomed this shift for whatever reason it was taking place, and God allowed the kindness to seep into me. I was grateful I didn't have the same experience that others had told me about.

People were so warm to us. One time, I was walking down the street, and it started to rain. I was pushing my three kids in their stroller, and we were caught out in the rain. People ran out of stores with umbrellas and gave them to us.

The sidewalks in Korea are not the best for big American strollers, let alone a triple seater. So, I tried running and pushing the stroller on an empty side street home to get out of the rain. One lady came up from behind and startled me at first, but she just wanted to help me push the stroller home. The street was on an incline, and it was hard to push up, but she grabbed the stroller and started running with me so we could make it home. I told her she didn't have to, but she did anyway.

People have all kinds of theories about why I was experiencing so much kindness when many others did not have similar experiences. I think that God allowed it. I might be a bridge, or my family might be a bridge for healing. But it's also tough to be that bridge if you have been burnt and broken. Perhaps God was making it go well—not only for me but for others through my life and story. I've had so many positive experiences I hope it will be the new norm and not the exception.

While I was in Korea, I met many women from the Korean mothers' group, and the lovely connections from the group became friends in real life. I wish people would know how we connected because I was told that I would never be in any Korean moms' circle. People don't typically mark the moments where love in friendship transcends race because they say, "Well, it should be like that." I don't want to let it slide by because even if it should be like that, it isn't always. I believe—and they believe—that true love transcends race. They so sweetly have allowed me in; I am grateful for that. Together, we formed this new word and world. It's called K-MOM, and it's a mother of a child of Korean descent, no matter what percent. If you're one drop Korean or your child is, you're in. That is the magic power that mothers have if they decide they want to change the world.

The way we connect despite race will actually change the world. Watch and see!

There must be a higher reason why I get along with all these Koreans so well. I never thought at this age that I would be making such close friends. I thought I was becoming a little more removed from people and okay with not having close friends. But I rely on these women; I really do. They boost me up. I'm even tearing up just writing about it. I can't believe I know such great women I respect so much, who do so much.

One thing that I can say about Koreans is that the older generation may not be so emotional as in wanting to hug and be all lovey-dovey, but they love their kids. They're good people. They're good fathers. They're good mothers. They're people of faith. They're kind. They're loving. It may not look like what everyone thinks as loving, but they're also super on excellence. They make me want to be more excellent, work harder, and achieve a certain kind of excellence—and that has nothing to do with a model minority. It has everything to do with their spirit.

But I also don't think that they always see their magic and power. They are these powerful, magical ladies. I see it, and I believe they are so wonderful. The best part is they feel I'm magic too, and they see the magic in me, and it allows us to look at each other and feel it together. It is the most special cultivated friendship of my life.

I'm super grateful to the internet, and I'm super thankful that all my life unfolded me into this group of women. Even after I left Korea, I kept meeting these women. I even met them in Los Angeles. I heard their stories, and we are sisters. We are one, and we redefined the term K-Mommy, didn't we, ummas? I'm so proud to be part of our group.

I ate my last *Busan milmyeon,* a cold flour starch noodle dish, on a pink stool before we left Busan. It is cold noodles in a light beef broth with sliced beef, pickled Korean radish, sesame seeds, seasoned dried laver, egg, garlic, some hot pepper paste, then topped with cucumber. The recipe is a local Busan take on another cold noodle dish called *naengmyeon,* also known as cold noodles. All these ingredients are placed in the center of the bowl in a light broth, which consists of part broth and part slushy ice flakes. It was marvelous, and every time I think of Busan, the taste comes to mind. I never came to eat any cold Korean noodle dish until the Korean introduced it to me. I came to truly understand the power of it when faced with Korean summer heat. That's when you say, "Ah yes, I understand its power," although there are also many dishes where you beat the heat with hot food. One such dish is *samgyetang,* a boiling chicken and ginseng soup made with whole young chicken because the meat is soft. The name *sam* refers to the ginger, *gye* is chicken, and *tang* is the soup. Other things found in the soup are garlic, ginger, jujubes, ginkgo nuts, chestnuts, and rice, all stuffed into the bird or placed in the soup. It is an aromatic treat and wonderful on a hot summer day. It is hard to understand why a hot soup helps until faced with the heat. Milmyeon in Busan, Naengmyeon, and Samgyetang are the icons of Korean summer.

I didn't want to leave, but when I did, I could firmly say I am well, and I was grateful. I believe there are a few stages to healing, the first of which happened to me in Korea, the calming of my body. With this calming and balancing of the mind and body, whatever you are striving for health-wise is easy, whether healing or weight loss. Most people forget to create the healing, calm space in the body first. So, they find that even when they are doing healthy things, their body doesn't absorb it; it rejects even healthy things. We stayed in Korea from spring into summer, and then we went to visit my sister in Hong Kong before returning to Busan for another few weeks in September 2019. Then we returned to the States. We decided that coming to Busan for spring and summer would become an annual tradition. Because of the air quality issues in Korea and the children being so young (Beau and Bijoo were three years old, and Baemin just turned two), we knew we could not be in Asia full time. Many times we thought, "Why don't we move here?" We felt so good there; everything fit. We prayed on it a lot, and then we decided that after all our travels, we wanted to pick a place that had the best elements of all the places we had been to or lived together. As we prayed, we remembered our dream and where we wanted to move to in our senior years. After all we had been through, we realized waiting to live our desire when we were old was no longer a plan we followed. We wanted to live fully and live *now*. It seemed clear that after thinking I wanted to die for all that time, what I wanted most was to live and love *now!*

A LITTLE BIRD

With all the lessons learned, I knew that I had to be in a place where I could ground myself and finish the healing that had begun in Korea—that and finish writing this story I have been telling you. There was one more piece to my dream as a single girl, and it was for my family to live at the beach.

We headed to Oahu, Hawaii, planning to try it for a few months. The Korean and I had honeymooned in Maui with the twins in my belly and promised each other that we would return to live there one day because of how we felt that trip. It would be perfect for escaping winter because I needed constant sun. While in Minnesota, my vitamin D levels had tanked, which has enormous effects on your well-being. I knew that to maintain a healthy balance, I never wanted to live far from shops that sold Korean food ingredients, and there's a lot of that in Oahu, including my dear H Mart. I learned H Mart now had more than eighty locations, with a new store about to open in Oahu. But the diversity of the island, not just Korean, pulled us here.

I felt an instant shift the moment we landed, and the fresh air and sun hit me as we began our first winter on Oahu. With my body at peace from our time in Korea, I started Halmoni's program anew earnestly with a deeper understanding. Two months in Oahu, I had already lost thirty pounds, much of which was gained from stress and medicine while I was ill, not pregnancy. My full energy began to return; just the way I moved felt right. The plan to come just for winter changed, and we never left.

One day in my beach bungalow, I heard a loud BANG! A bird had flown into the glass door of our lanai. When I realized it was a bird, I was concerned it was dead. I tried to get close to check, and it fluttered back to life. It was stunned and hurt but attempted to fly away.

There were other birds that seemed like its family. They were worried and urgently chirping for it to fly away. I only wanted to help, but it was scared. It took off for a short distance and fell a few times, but the family flew alongside and guided it up into a tree.

Two days later, the bird came back. It perched on top of my lanai fence and stared at me intently. It was closer to me than I ever have been to a bird in the wild. It looked me dead in the eye, and we had a moment. It felt like a thousand years passed before it flew off. Its wings were healed. That's when I realized that bird was me, and I knew I was going to be okay.

CREDITS

Editors
Dawn Greer
J.B Yoon

Cover Designer- Haroula Kontorousi
Interior Formatter- Davor Dramikanin
Illustration Cover- Bridget M Sidden
Author Manager- Sarah Duckworth
Branding- Hope Rippere

Special thanks to: Susan Strecker, Michael Allen and
Angela Walker.

ACKNOWLEDGMENTS

First and always, Ruth Bamela Engo Tjega, my mum, for your consistent love and mentoring in motherhood. Thank you, Mum. You are everything to me.

I want to thank my husband, who taught me about what it means to be in love and stay there.

To my children Hyung-Beau, Bijoo-Ruth, and Baemin Yoon, the most beautiful and inspiring people I have ever met. Thanks for all the fun baby loves and for your loving support of umma.

The creators of the Korean Mommies group, Lina Olivia Kim and Cathy Meilak, and their admin team.

Jenny Kim of Parenthood Together group, thank you.

My friend Luci Kim for her encouraging me and reading my book first.

Greta Cavazzoni Carrano for an enduring friendship that supported me professionally and personally for two decades.

Monica Gambee for a million mothering messages.

To Chef Marja Vongerichten and Jean-Georges Vongerichten for their PBS program *Kimchi Chronicles,* and to Marja for being even kinder in real life than on television.

To Nelly Moudime for always showing us that being black is beautiful and to celebrate that.

To Ted Gibson and Jason Backe, who supported my foundation with their talent and always pointed me to moving forward and starring in my own life.

To all my friends and family on Facebook, especially my Korean adoptee friends and my Korean Cooking Friends group.

Ghylian Bell and Blossette Kitson, my African American mothers.

To my Louisiana family, the Helm family: Abigail, Anna, and Ms. Carol, love y'all forever.

The executives who worked at MTV who guided my path and gave me opportunities: Ian Rowe, Christina Norman, Stephen Friedman, Jason Rzepka, Georgia Arnold, Steven Kolb (now at the CFDA), and Former Chairman Bill Roedy.

To Sonya Lockett for her support when at BET.

To Steve Villano of Cable Positive and the late Jack Valenti for telling me "canceled" doesn't mean "over."

The MAC AIDS fund for supporting my work from Mr. John Demsey to Craig Cichy and the makeup artists, Romero Jennings in particular.

To Liz Agbortabi Oton for making Cameroon and me feel so proud.

For Marian Lee Dicus and Jeanne Sun, who reminded me that sisterhood can come in the most peculiar and amazing ways.

Thank you to the United Nations for a magical upbringing.

Thank you designer Marc Bouwer and Paul Margolin for endless kindness.

To Maggie Rizer for helping me own my name.

To Sally Morrison, who listens and empowered me as an African girl wanting to tackle African issues.

The late UN Secretary-General Kofi Annan, who remained kind in power and always kind to me, and Mrs. Nane Annan for writing the letter that got everyone to believe the NY AIDS FILM FESTIVAL should be.

UNAIDS family Bertil Lindbladt, Djibril Diallo, and Victor Mari Ortega.

The members of the board of African Action on AIDS.

Lastly, I would like to thank my family:

My father, the late Paul Bamela Engo.

Paul Bamela Engo Junior.

Vivek and Barbara Engo Aranha, along with Sophie and Adele.

Babs, your sisterhood means so much to me. Thanks for helping me when I fell down and reminding me that slowly but surely, I would get back up.

Zahra Giles always inspires me to open my heart and braid my hair.

Pamela and Teresa Engo for showing up when I was sick.

To Juhee and Stephanie for helping with the children at my most vulnerable moment.

The Tjega family: Lidia, Simon, Pauline, Louise, Pauline, Teclaire, and Paul, and all my cousins and their children. Without your love, my creativity and belief in myself would be nonexistent.

To Dr. Dong Shik Yoon, Jo Sook Yoon, Byongsuk "Billyoonaire" Yoon, and So Young Yoon for welcoming me so graciously into the Yoon family.

To H Mart for creating a company to support the Korean community that saved my life with Korean food.

Finally, to the Halmoni who changed my life that day in H Mart. You are not in my sight but remain in my heart forever. Thank you!

Thank you all. See you at the house by the sea. All Glory be to God

ABOUT THE AUTHOR

AFRICA BYONGCHAN YOON

Africa Yoon is an author, television host, and celebrated activist known for working with young people on education, poverty eradication, racism, at-risk youth, obesity, bullying, sexual health, and sport. She was awarded the Golden Graal humanitarian prize in Rome for using film and television to educate about HIV/AIDS and named one of the Top 40 Youth Activists globally by MTV and the Kaiser Family Foundation in her late teens. She has spoken worldwide, including at the United Nations, and is recognized for ending her speeches in song and dance. A graduate of New York University/Tisch School of the Arts, Mrs. Yoon bridges culture, activism, and entertainment in all her projects.

Born into a family of diplomats, including an Olympian-turned-United Nations-ambassador-father and activist mother, she is currently the CEO of Blackyoonicorn, a mommy and me cultural company that sells language and cultural toys for children and affordable luxury global home goods for their mothers. With a passion for Korean food and health, she runs the popular "Korean Cooking Friends" Facebook Group and cooking app by the same name. Mrs. Yoon lives in Oahu, Hawaii, with her husband and children and splits her time in Busan, South Korea.